IT'S A
BABY
GIRL!

IT'S A BABY GIRL!

*The Unique Wonder and
Special Nature of Your Daughter
from Pregnancy to Two Years*

The Gurian Institute

Stacie Bering, MD, and
Adie Goldberg, ACSW, MEd

FOREWORD BY MICHAEL GURIAN

JOSSEY-BASS
A Wiley Imprint
www.josseybass.com

Published by Jossey-Bass
A Wiley Imprint
989 Market Street, San Francisco, CA 94103-1741—www.josseybass.com

Jossey-Bass books and products are available through most bookstores. To contact Jossey-Bass directly call our Customer Care Department within the U.S. at 800-956-7739, outside the U.S. at 317-572-3986, or fax 317-572-4002.

Jossey-Bass also publishes its books in a variety of electronic formats. Some content that appears in print may not be available in electronic books.

All names and circumstances have been changed for the book's stories.

Library of Congress Cataloging-in-Publication Data
Bering, Stacie, date.
  It's a baby girl! : the unique wonder and special nature of your daughter from pregnancy to two years / Stacie Bering and Adie Goldberg ; foreword by Michael Gurian. — 1st ed.
    p. cm.
  Includes bibliographical references and index.
  ISBN 978-0-470-24339-8 (pbk.)
  1. Infant girls—Development. 2. Infant girls—Care. 3. Infants—Development. 4. Toddlers—Development. 5. Girls. I. Goldberg, Adie, date. II. Title. III. Title: It is a baby girl.
  HQ774.B445 2009
  305.232082—dc22

                                                                                2008031670

Printed in the United States of America
FIRST EDITION
PB Printing   10 9 8 7 6 5 4 3 2 1

Contents

Foreword

Congratulations! You have a brand new baby girl!

Having a baby girl will change your lives in beautiful ways that you could not have imagined until now. With your new baby girl in your arms, your home, your relationships, your day-to-day existence will flower as they never have before. To have such a child is to experience ecstatic joy and humbling awe at the miracles inherent in the universe.

As with every great thing in life, however, having a new baby girl presents challenges. Before you had your daughter, people may have smiled, "Life will never be the same!" Now here you are—life will never be the same . . . and a little help would be nice!

If you have received or picked up this book, you might be wondering

- How does one care for a baby girl in particular?
- What does this young daughter need?
- What are key developmental moments in her life?
- What are accurate expectations for her development?
- How are her needs the same as any child, and yet, also, unique to her as an individual *girl*?

All of us at the Gurian Institute are devoted to providing science-based and life-affirming answers to parents' questions about how to raise their children. In this book, you'll find information, wisdom, stories, and fascinating science about your developing girl.

Dr. Stacie Bering, an obstetrician who specializes in women's health and child development, and Adie Goldberg, a clinical social worker who specializes in early childhood education, have culled through the best new literature (and best old wisdom) on raising girls in order to bring you this book. They have also infused this book with their own personal experience with patients. Between them, Dr. Bering and Ms. Goldberg have sixty years' experience in helping families of young children.

Along with their experience and understanding, Dr. Bering and Ms. Goldberg are also Certified Gurian Institute Trainers. Thus they specialize in helping parents understand the individual needs of *girls* and *boys*. Boys and girls are similar, but they are also different. I hope as you read this book, you'll be intrigued by how wonderfully similar and different they are.

Enjoy this book and enjoy your beautiful girl. If you can, share comments with us on www.gurianinstitute.com. We look forward to hearing about how your daughter is flourishing. The world needs her passion and purpose, and I know she will make you proud!

—Michael Gurian, president, the Gurian Institute

From generation to generation.
To Jeffry, Cassie, and Zack,
Emily, Maggie, Chloe, and Robb,
and
the families who have entrusted their stories to us.

Acknowledgments

Baby girls grow best when there are more than their two loving parents involved in their care. Families thrive in a circle of support. This is the case when it comes to writing books as well.

Michael Gurian is at the core of the professional circle of this book. Last summer the phone rang and it was Michael. He said he had an opportunity. When Michael calls with an opportunity there is usually growth and a fair bit of work involved. Writing this book and its companion book for boys was just such an opportunity. Michael has a passion for making sure that girls, boys, and their parents are supported and informed as they embark on the parenting journey. We cannot begin to thank Michael for the advice, inspiration, and guidance he has freely given us. His generosity has not gone unnoticed.

However, vision alone does not sustain the writing of a book. Alan Rinzler, our editor at Jossey-Bass, assisted by his editorial team of Carol Hartland, Nana Twumasi, and Donna Cohn, moved us and the project forward with his editorial expertise. He has been more than patient with a pair of first-time authors. We have learned much under his tutelage and we can truly say that we are stronger writers at the conclusion of this project.

Over twenty years ago we began working together at Woman-Health, an OB-GYN clinic. Women came to us to share their concerns, fears, and dreams for and about their children. We offered advice despite the fact that we were still without children of our own. Five children later, we are wiser and humbled. We offer a special thank-you to the patients of WomanHealth who shared their lives with us. The staff at WomanHealth were patient with us over countless lunches. Their good humor sustained us, and their stories have made us both laugh and cry.

Pam Silverstein was the founding physician of WomanHealth. Her husband, Steve, and their children, Shayna and Josh, completed our families' circle of support. We both cherish their wisdom, love, and loyalty, especially during this writing process.

Please indulge us for a moment as we acknowledge our own families, for they have taught us more than all the collected years of postgraduate education between us. Stacie would like to thank Jeffry Finer, without whom she would never have known the joy of parenthood, and her two children, Cassie and Zachary, who, even as young adults, continue to guide her in this on-the-job training that is the true nature of being a parent.

Adie would like to thank Robb for his computer knowledge, patience with the writing process, and his ability to still make her laugh at the end of the day. To her daughters, Emily and Maggie, who listened *ad nauseam* long distance, gave feedback on early drafts, and asked questions that continue to make their mother think, a mother's thank-you and love. A special thank-you to Chloe, who, as the last of the littermates still at home, was asked to be the most patient with us as we wrote this book. She served as our memory bank, reminding us of stories long forgotten.

Our thank-you to each of our readers. You will continue to teach us and remind us that there is always much to learn.

Stacie Bering, MD
Adie Goldberg, ACSW, MEd

Introduction:
It's a Baby Girl!

Congratulations! It's a girl!

From the moment you found out you were pregnant, the wondering began. Healthy? Blond or brunette? Musician or scientist? Your family's athleticism or your husband Harold's sense of humor? Boy or girl?

You and Harold had the name list pared down to three of each. Your Aunt Tillie predicted a girl from the way you were carrying the baby and your neighbor confirms the prediction when she noted your craving for sweets. The next few months and years will reveal the answers to many of your questions, but the wonders of twenty-first century medicine have officially ended the gender-guessing game.

The reason you know now is that you are thirty-five years old. Your doctor ordered an amniocentesis to be performed at week sixteen of your pregnancy due to "advanced maternal age" (a phrase most pregnant women detest!). He explains that mothers over the age of thirty-five are at increased risk for carrying a child with Down syndrome or other rarer chromosomal abnormalities. At the time of the amniocentesis you were asked if you want to know the sex of your baby. At week eighteen, your obstetrician's office calls with the results—a chromosomally healthy baby girl!

If you didn't have an amnio, you might have discovered your baby's gender at an eighteen-week ultrasound. With advances in

1

technology and the ready availability of ultrasound machines, your doctor or midwife often orders a routine ultrasound during your second trimester to make sure that your baby is developing normally and that your due date is accurate. On that magical day, the sonographer shows you a beating heart, two arms, and two legs which happen to be spread apart so that you and your partner detect two unmistakable swellings (your daughter's labia) between them.

Then again, you might have found out the old-fashioned way, seconds after giving birth, still gasping for breath, when your doctor announced, "It's a girl!"

Whatever way you heard the news, we want you to know there's a lot more brewing in your daughter's body than the sugar and spice of nursery rhyme fame. It's an exciting world of hormones, brain structure, and genetic propensities.

Welcome to the exciting world of parenting a daughter!

Since the birth of your new daughter, well-meaning family and friends have been full of special advice about girls, from the strange and mysterious to the clichés of conventional wisdom. You may have heard that

- Your daughter will be easier to diaper because you don't have to point any anatomy downwards before fastening the tabs.
- Your daughter will be more dependent and less rebellious than a boy.
- Your daughter will be more emotionally expressive and complex than a boy.

And just when you breathe a sigh of relief, the experienced parent of a grown-up girl will remind you, "Just wait until your daughter is a teenager!"

Baby Girl Story

Rebeka walked into Sunday school, carrying her sobbing fourteen-month-old daughter as she sent her five-year-old son Joel off to the kindergarten classroom. Liz, another mother in the waiting area, turned to console her. Rebeka said, "I don't get it. I majored in developmental psychology and I haven't raised Susie any differently than I raised Joel. When he was mad at me, he'd pinch, throw things, and slap. He expressed his frustration with his body. Susie sobs these crocodile tears and seems to hold a grudge even though she's too young to know what a grudge is!"

Girls Really Are Different from Boys

The latest research, using the most up-to-date technological hardware for scanning brains while the body acts, has shown us what role the gender of a brain plays in impacting human behavior. We have solid evidence that your daughter's brain structure, genetic predisposition, and hormonal development all play a critical role in shaping your woman-to-be.

Your daughter's girl brain, her body's CEO, has been under a different set of construction plans than her brother's since a few weeks following conception. As a result, your daughter will process information differently, perceive the world differently, respond with different behaviors, and set different priorities from her male sibling.

Even though common wisdom tells us it is a woman's prerogative to change her mind, one thing is for sure; by birth your daughter has already made up hers and it's definitely the mind of a girl.

Advances in science have enabled researchers to peer deep inside the brain and actually film it while a subject is thinking and processing information, giving them new insights into how differently the genders store memories, make decisions, and solve problems.

Magnetic Resonance Images or MRIs (detailed pictures of the internal organs) are now able to map the human brain. Researchers have literally seen what we have always known. There are fundamental gender differences and they start in the very structure of the human brain. Studies show that males and females process information, listen, and experience events in very different ways. Functional MRIs (fMRIs) indicate which areas of your daughter's brain are activated during various activities and events. Catch her brother doing the same activity and his MRI will often give us a very different picture.

What's even more interesting is that if we took a slice of your daughter's brain we wouldn't be able to tell her race, ethnicity, or religion.

We could, however, confirm that this is a female brain!

Here's what else we know about the differences between baby girls and baby boys at birth:

• Before you bring your daughter home from the hospital, the charge nurse in the nursery will be able to point out that she focuses longer on the talking faces around her than does the newborn boy in the layette next to her.

• Your daughter will simultaneously use both hemispheres of her more connected brain. There's greater blood flow between the two sides of your daughter's brain and as a result, she may be better able than her male cousin to multitask early in life.

• The newborn girls in the nursery feel more pain and discomfort than the blue-capped boys lying next to them, and they will let the nurses know it. And if someone drops a metal pan in the nursery, those same girls may cry out in irritation. If, however, one of those boys finally does get disturbed, it may be your daughter who is easier to soothe with soft cooing and gentle jiggling.

• Your girl baby has a differently shaped pelvis than the boys in the nursery, more body fat from the get-go, and a different way of processing oxygen in her muscles. This may give her less stamina than her male counterparts later on in life, but at least at the start, your daughter is in fact the hardier and healthier sex.

● BABY GIRL BRAIN FACT ●
Different from Birth

Doctors say, "A newborn girl is the physiological equivalent of a four- to six-week-old boy." This difference is due to the genetic make up of boys and girls. Two Xs are, at least *in utero* and at birth, better than one. The X chromosome carries immunity factors, and the female infant's chances of survival are increased by having two X chromosomes. If there's a problem with one, she has an alternative to draw from.

Despite the reassurances that, in the beginning, girls may be queen of the survival mountain, you may still feel insecure, confused, and consumed with worry. You have important questions. The playpens, formula, and rigid feeding schedules that your parents and grandparents swore by are remnants of the past. You are raising a daughter just at a time when there has been an explosion of brain research with scientific advances. What are you supposed to do with all that information?

● **BABY GIRL BRAIN FACT** ●

A More Connected Brain

Unlike males, females rarely experience *in utero* hits of testosterone that shrink the developing centers for communication, observation, and processing of emotion in the fetal brain. As a result, a girl's potential to develop skills in these areas are better at birth than a boy's. A girl's brain sprouts more connections in these areas. Because of her larger communication center, your daughter will most likely grow up to use more words than her brother.

How This Book Works

As a parent of a girl, you'll find this book is designed to help you navigate the journey of your daughter's unique brain structure that is made up of sugar and spice, estrogen, and everything nice.

Some of the journey may surprise you. For example, our friend Liz came into work one day frustrated, trying to figure out what Julie, now ten months old, wanted. Julie had let Liz know from the beginning that she wouldn't tolerate a wet diaper. She wouldn't stop crying until Liz dried her thoroughly after her bath. This morning, a new behavior emerged. Every time her bib was wet with cereal or milk spilled from her tippy cup, she screamed until Liz produced a clean one. By the third bib, Julie was done eating and Liz began to wonder what she had done wrong in her attempt to raise a resilient little girl.

Don't worry if this happens to you, too. We hope this book will help you be the best parent possible to your baby girl as she starts out in the world. We don't intend it to be the complete guide or last word on all the details of baby care, but what is special and unique about this book is that we can tell you what's unique about having a daughter. Each chapter contains boxes which include real-life "Baby Girl Stories" and "Baby Girl Brain Facts," with the latest in scientific information and professional advice.

So here's how it works:

Chapter One will guide you through the biology of your pregnancy. You will discover how DNA and hormones interact to shape a girl's development. We'll try to demystify the secret drama of human chromosomes, genes, and brain development that unfolds *in utero*. In addition to looking at what is going on with your daughter, we'll update you on the most recent research regarding nutrition, the effects of hyper-stimulating the fetus, the impact of stress, the use of alcohol, drugs, and nicotine, and the role of exercise during pregnancy.

Chapter Two begins with a quick review of how biology and environment work together during the first year of your daughter's life. Every sensory experience your newborn has is shaping the way your girl's brain circuits are being wired. Each time your daughter has a new experience, she is creating new connections in her brain. Each experience, like an electrical signal, passes on a message. The more messages, the more repetition, and eventually neural roads form. Through this process, learning is taking place and her brain becomes "hardwired."

For years, folks have debated the role of nurture versus nature in the shaping of a newborn. Many favored the importance of nurturing, arguing that people are molded by the outside influences on their brains. The pressure can be overwhelming for parents who struggle with the potential power of this type of influence. Advances in brain research and neuroscience, however, have given us evidence that your daughter's brain has its own nature, that it's programmed by genes and evolution to function in a certain way, and that much of this will happen no matter what environmental influences you bring to bear.

Baby Girl Story

Kathleen, a successful physician in a male-dominated specialty, grew up in a family with two older brothers, seven and nine years older than she. She has two elementary school-age sons and an 18-month-old daughter, Morgan. A chess set has been on her coffee table since her boys were toddlers. Her boys now play competitive chess. However, as toddlers, they would stack the chess pieces into mountains before knocking them over. She spoke with genuine surprise as she described her daughter's reaction to the chess set. "Morgan creates chess piece families with a mommy chess piece, a daddy piece, and lots of baby pawns. I sort of got used to picking up the pieces after all the boys' stacking."

Chapter Two concludes with brain-building activities for your girl, parenting tips for you, a summary of developmental highlights, and a final note for dads.

The brain chemistry that was set in motion and described in the first two chapters doesn't end there, however. Chapter Three looks at what lies ahead for your daughter and what you can do to facilitate her full development.

Why do boys and girls as a group play differently? Your daughter will more often than not be found in the cooperative and less competitive play area of her preschool. The boys may be searching out physical play. The first section of Chapter Three focuses on the full range of girls' play, toys, and friendships. Not all girls turn every inanimate object into a baby. Your daughter might be happiest outside with the boys kicking a soccer ball around. We'll help you identify what is the range of normal, what skills your daughter needs in order to play, as well as provide parenting pointers to help build success for the future.

The last section of Chapter Three presents what to look for academically when it comes to your daughter. Parents and experts weigh in on how to pick a preschool or day-care provider and on the specific learning and attachment needs of girls during these preschool years.

Finally, Chapter Four will help you realize that you are not alone. This chapter helps you identify and locate your sources of support. Sometimes we need to be reminded that our relationships with our partner, extended family, and ourselves are resources and need as much nurturing during this time as our little angel.

This chapter ends with a look at how mothers and fathers parent differently. We'll let biology explain why the testosterone coursing through a father's body may make him more comfortable with a daughters' risk taking. With a mother's female brain wired for connection, she may want to pull her daughters closer.

There will be differences. There will be difficulties. There will be great joy. We promise that no matter what your gender, you will laugh more, cry more, and love more than you ever have before. We hope this book helps you both enjoy your baby girl and relax as you begin the incredible ride that's ahead!

The Girl
Inside You

Sara was waiting for her amniocentesis results. An obstetrician herself, she knew how long the test took to perform, so she was expecting a call from the genetics clinic any day. At thirty-five, she was considered an "elderly primigravida," a phrase she used wryly as she described older first-time moms like herself.

Because of her age, she knew she had a higher risk of having a child with a genetic problem, and so she had chosen to have an amniocentesis. This involved taking a small amount of fluid from around her baby and checking to see that everything was OK.

Finally, the call came.

"We've got your results back," Ginger, the counselor at the genetics clinic told Sara. "The chromosomes are normal. Everything looks fine."

But there was something Ginger had left out.

"What is it?" Sara asked, her stomach doing silly flip-flops. She couldn't explain it, but she wanted a girl, and Ginger, her close friend, knew it.

"Why, it's a girl of course!"

Perhaps, like Sara, you have the results of your amniocentesis, or the ultrasonographer saw the two swellings that identified your daughter's labia at a routine ultrasound. Perhaps this is your first baby and you weren't worried about what sex your baby was. When curious friends asked, "Do you want a boy or a girl?" you replied, "Either, as long as it's healthy," and now you are holding her in your arms. She has just drifted off to sleep so you're trying to read a few pages.

Then again, maybe like Sara, you were hoping for a girl.

Some couples might wonder if it's possible to choose the sex of their baby. Perhaps you have two boys and wanted the experience of having a daughter. You might have asked if there was any way to increase your chances of having a girl. Science comes back with a resounding "NO!"

● **BABY GIRL BRAIN FACT** ●

Why Does a Doctor Suggest an Amniocentesis?

- You're thirty-five or older and the risk of Down syndrome and other, rarer, chromosomal abnormalities, increases with age. Down syndrome is the result of a baby having an extra chromosome.
- You had a blood test called a triple or quadruple screen at week sixteen of your pregnancy and the results were abnormal. With an abnormal result you are at increased risk for delivering a child with Down syndrome, a spinal defect (spina bifida), or a severe brain abnormality. REMEMBER! It is quite common to have a false positive result. Usually it comes from you or your doctor mis-calculating your due date. An amniocentesis and an ultrasound will give you a more accurate result.
- You had an ultrasound, and something abnormal was detected.
- You have a history of a chromosomal abnormality in your family.
- You have already delivered a child with a chromosomal abnormality.

● BABY GIRL BRAIN FACT ●
Guaranteeing a Girl, or "Wear the Jockeys,
Not the Boxers, Honey!"

Depending on the myth, you should
- Eat lots of vegetables and fish; have chocolate for dessert
- Make love in the afternoon
- Make love on even numbered days
- Make love during the full moon
- Have the female partner initiate sex
- Be sure the male partner has an orgasm first
- Make sure your husband keeps his genitals warm by wearing close-fitting underwear and tight trousers
- Put a pink ribbon under your pillow and a wooden spoon under your bed

Remember:
- All of these suggestions are myths.
- None has held up to scientific scrutiny.
- But the odds are pretty good no matter what you do—you have about a fifty-fifty chance of conceiving a girl!

However you made your girl, you're about to find out how genes, DNA, and chromosomes worked together to create your baby girl and what scientists are learning about why your daughter is so different from your best friend's son, starting from the moment of conception.

If you're curious to know why your friends and family are telling you that girls are unique, read on!

Gene Talk

1. What is DNA? The body is made up of different kinds of cells: liver cells, skin cells, and blood cells, to name a few. DNA is every cell's set of instructions or blueprint. It tells the cell whether it's going to help your little girl taste chocolate or help her do push-ups.

2. What are genes, anyway? Genes are made up of the DNA. They are the instruction manual for your girl's body. They tell her body how to develop and function. Genes determine whether your daughter will grow tall and slender like Uncle Fred or short and squat like Aunt Pearl. Your daughter's genes determine whether she'll have high blood pressure or a tendency toward diabetes. Your daughter has an estimated twenty-five thousand genes.

3. What's a chromosome and where can you find one? In the center of most of your body's cells, you'll find the nucleus, or the cell's command center. Within that nucleus are the chromosomes, the gene holders of your body. Chromosomes come in pairs, like shoes. We each have twenty-three pairs. When you and your partner created your daughter, you each gave her half of the set of twenty-three chromosomes.

4. What makes my girl a girl? Blame it on the sex chromosomes, specifically two X chromosomes. Because all of Mom's cells have two X chromosomes, her eggs will always pass on an X chromosome to her child, male or female. But Dad has two different sex chromosomes, the long and lean X chromosome and the rather puny Y chromosome. Half his sperm will carry an X chromosome, the other half a Y. Your daughter was created when an X-carrying sperm met up with Mom's egg (always carrying an X chromosome). Human girls are XX.

Although your daughter's X chromosomes are long and lean, containing up to fourteen hundred genes, she missed out on one important gene (important to guys, that is) that appears only on that stubby boy-making Y chromosome. It's called SRY and it directs other genes on other chromosomes to get involved in making boy parts, starting off with the all-important testosterone-producing testicles.

● **BABY GIRL BRAIN FACT** ●
A Lot of Neural Mileage

Your daughter's forty-six chromosomes contain so much information that if you wrote it all down, the data would fill a stack of books two hundred feet high! If you pulled the entire twisted DNA from a single cell and stretched it out, it would be as long as a car. If you stretched out all the DNA in a human body, it would stretch to the sun and back six hundred times!

Without the SRY gene, the collection of cells that became your daughter had no choice but to go on its default path—that of the female. Or so it's long been thought. As scientists begin to unlock the secrets of the human genetic code, they are beginning to find evidence that there are ovary-determining genes on the X chromosome.

Without the influence of testosterone coming from a pair of testicles, your daughter's early collection of cells is propelled down a path that is uniquely female.

From Embryo to Baby Girl

Your baby's journey to becoming a girl child started when your husband's X sperm fertilized your X-bearing egg. Initially, the embryo had a "unisex" look about it. If you were able to peek in at that moment you wouldn't have been able to tell if you were having a boy or girl.

Toward the end of your first trimester, your daughter began stage one of the three stages of development that made her a girl. First her ovaries formed. Next came her other internal girl parts, her uterus and fallopian tubes. Finally her vagina and external organs made their appearance.

Step 1: Formation of the ovaries. At about week ten of your pregnancy, your daughter's ovaries began to develop per her genetic plan. While your best friend's fetal boy was inundated with hits of testosterone, your daughter's ovaries were not making much of a contribution to the huge amounts of estrogen that pour out of your placenta. At least *in utero,* estrogen does not drive your daughter's female development. That will happen shortly after birth.

Step 2: Formation of her internal female organs. Just like her male counterpart, your daughter started off with two sets of cords in her abdomen. The Mullerian ducts were the female set and were free to grow because there was no SRY gene to stop them. These ducts were destined to become her uterus, fallopian tubes, and the upper part of the vagina. The Wolffian ducts, which would have grown into boy parts, wither away, unused.

Step 3: Her external girl parts. Up until about eleven to twelve weeks of pregnancy, your daughter's genital area was rather nondescript. There was nothing on the outside that could tell you if this was a boy or a girl. Even though female hormones will be held responsible for much about your daughter's future female development and behavior, it is her female genetic code, not her hormones, driving the growth of her clitoris, labia, and lower vagina.

You Can't Blame It on Her Hormones

Your daughter's ovaries are not doing much in the way of producing estrogen *in utero,* thus her journey to womanhood, at least before birth, is determined by girl-promoting genes, unhindered by a Y chromosome's interference. Without the stormy hits of testosterone your nephew was exposed to, your daughter's reproductive anatomy develops in a leisurely fashion. Your daughter won't experience her "hits" of estrogen until she is out of your body.

The first series comes shortly after birth, and lasts for the first six months of life, continuing the work that began *in utero.* During this time your daughter's ovaries begin producing estrogen at levels not seen again until she is an adult. Her female brain circuitry soaks in this bath of female hormones. At the same time, these estrogen hits take responsibility for getting your daughter's reproductive structures ready for her to make babies of her own. Yes, we know that seems eons away!

The second hit of estrogen comes with puberty. This sets the processes in motion that will change your girl's body into that of a woman. Starting a few years before your daughter actually gets her first period, her stick-straight girl body will gradually develop curves, and grow underarm and pubic hair. Her breasts will emerge, and she'll probably complain that they hurt.

Without testosterone interfering, your daughter developed not only female genitalia but a decidedly female brain. Estrogen will later be the hormone responsible for the physical changes your daughter will experience, but in the meantime it is your daughter's girl brain that will direct her female approach to the world.

Is Your Girl's Brain Different from Her Brother's?

Yes. Absolutely.

The latest research shows that testosterone and its buddies have profound effects on the formation of the male fetal brain. Put testosterone in the mix and some cells in some areas are destroyed while other areas of the uniquely male brain, generally less verbally and emotionally oriented, develop. Without testosterone your girl's communication and emotion centers develop unperturbed.

In the early days of your pregnancy we were unable to differentiate between a male and a female embryo's genitalia. We also wouldn't be able to differentiate between a male and female brain. We all start out the same. But even before you missed your period, your daughter's nervous system was beginning on its complicated path.

How Does a Baby Girl's Brain Grow?

By the time you had taken an early pregnancy test and gotten the news, your daughter's brain was starting to form. Your baby was little more than a tiny flat disk floating over a ball of cells. The transformation of this fertilized blob of chemically driven cells into a young woman who will solve complex problems, talk on the phone for hours, and read chemistry textbooks is an amazing process.

A microscopic groove developed along the length of the tiny disk. The groove deepened and eventually sealed its edges over to form a long tube, called the neural tube. By five weeks, the organ that looked like a lumpy inchworm had already embarked on the most spectacular feat of human development: the creation of the deeply creased cerebral cortex, the part of the brain that will eventually allow your daughter to move, think, speak, plan, and create. The brain of your growing girl changes so much over the next thirty-four weeks that researchers are able to tell you how many weeks pregnant you are by looking at your daughter's brain!

● BABY GIRL BRAIN FACT ●
Brain Space

At birth, girls' brains on average are smaller than boys' brains. Your daughter will have the same number of neurons as a boy, but she will jam more into less space, the female brain's equivalent of wearing a girdle!

What's Unique About a Baby Girl's Brain?
Your daughter's brain will perform millions of tasks in a uniquely female way.

Without the influence of the Y chromosome, the fetal girl brain takes on the structure and function of a female brain. Some areas of her brain will be larger than in a boy's brain, others smaller. In certain areas of her brain, there will be more connections between brain cells than in a boy's brain.

Her brain will

- Control her body temperature, blood pressure, heart rate, and breathing

- Translate a flood of information about the world around her from her eyes, ears, nose, and taste buds
- Regulate her physical motion when walking, talking, standing, or sitting
- Think, dream, reason, and experience emotions

And this is all done by an organ that is about the size of a small grapefruit!

A Quick Tour of the Baby Girl Brain
The key players in your daughter's brain are

1. The cerebrum. The biggest part of the brain is the cerebrum, also called the cerebral hemispheres. Most of the brain's weight, 85 percent, is devoted to the cerebrum. The cerebrum is the seat of higher brain functions—thinking, reasoning, speaking, and interpreting the environment. Memories are stored here, and emotions processed. When your daughter starts to crawl, her cerebrum will tell her arms and legs what to do.

2. Cerebellum. The cerebellum is at the back of the brain, below the cerebrum. Although a lot smaller than the cerebrum, only one-eighth of its size, the cerebellum is a very important part of the brain. It controls balance, movement, and coordination (how your muscles work together). Because of your daughter's cerebellum, she will be able to stand upright, keep her balance, and spin circles through her world.

3. Brain stem. Another small but mighty brain part is the brain stem, which sits beneath the cerebrum, in front of the cerebellum. The brain stem connects the brain to the spinal cord and is in charge of all the basic functions your girl's body needs to stay alive—breathing air, digesting food, and circulating blood.

4. Pituitary gland. The pea-sized, powerful pituitary gland is in charge of making your girl grow large by producing and releasing growth hormones into her body.

5. Hypothalamus. Last, but certainly not least, is the hypothalamus, the brain's regulator of emotions, body temperature, and food and water intake. At some point your daughter will tell you to stop putting a coat on her because YOU are cold—and you can thank her hypothalamus for that!

How Does a Tube Turn into a Brain?

The neural tube (the sealed-off collection of early cells) starts to imitate a pretzel by swelling, folding, and contorting to form the various parts of the brain. It divides into the forebrain, midbrain, and hindbrain. This tube's divisions turn into the brain parts listed above. Your little girl's eyes and nose will develop from the division of the neural tube that became the forebrain. This area also develops into the cerebrum and the hypothalamus. The midbrain is destined to become the brainstem. The hindbrain will become the cerebellum. Your daughter's brain is growing rapidly at this point. If you were looking in on her now, you would be struck by her odd look. She's almost all head!

Inside the tube, the cells divide rapidly and cause the tube to thicken. Some of these cells become neurons or nerve cells. Neurons are initially produced in the central canal of the neural tube. Although they are born there, they don't stay put and will migrate to their final destination in the brain. These cells collect together to form the different centers of the brain and spinal cord, and they send out axons, long, threadlike extensions that connect with other nerves.

At nine weeks, the embryo's ballooning brain allows your daughter to bend her body, hiccup, and react to loud sounds.

By week ten your girl's brain is producing almost 250,000 new neurons every minute!

By your second trimester the grooves and furrows of your daughter's brain begin developing. Nature takes advantage of these peaks and valleys to cram as many neurons as possible into a relatively small space.

By forty weeks, or term, your daughter's brain is an engineering masterpiece!

Is Your "Girl Pregnancy" Different from a "Boy Pregnancy"?

Yes, but you're not likely to notice. Here's what researchers have found so far:

• Even though a boy fetus may move around more *in utero,* your girl fetus is moving her mouth more than her male counterparts. This early practice prepares your daughter for the future hours on her cell phone!

• Feeling nauseated? Girl pregnancies produce more of the pregnancy hormone hCG. Researchers think high levels of hCG might be related to a severe form of morning sickness called hyperemesis.

• At each week of pregnancy, girls weigh less than boys, so that when they're born, girls weigh on average a half pound less than boys. Their heads are smaller, and they're shorter than the boys. Those little heads are easier to deliver and you are less likely to need a C-section.

● BABY GIRL BRAIN FACT ●
The Old Wives Weigh In

Here's some wisdom from a time-honored source—"The Old Wives"—and they say you're carrying a girl if

- Your baby's heart rate is more than 140 beats per minute.
- Your husband gains weight during your pregnancy.
- You're carrying the baby high.
- You're moody.
- Your hands are softer than when you weren't pregnant.
- You crave chocolate.
- You break out with acne.

We're still learning what makes girl pregnancies different from boy pregnancies. It's an active area of research, so stay tuned!

Will My Girl Be Okay? Ten Simple Things to Do

Now that you're pregnant, you're probably paying closer attention to your diet. Getting the right nutrients is not only important for your little one's health—it can affect her intelligence too. Certain foods positively affect your girl's memory and capacity to learn, and others can hinder proper brain development. These smart moves will help you maximize your future Madame Curie's learning.

1. First of all, strive to gain the right amount of weight. Obstetricians recommend that women of normal weight gain between twenty-five and thirty-five pounds during their pregnancy. A study from the National Institutes of Health found that women who follow that prescription have children with higher IQs than kids born to moms who gained more or less weight during their pregnancy. This is sort of a domino effect, as your prenatal weight gain affects your baby's birth weight, which, in turn, affects his brain size and IQ. Gaining too much or too little weight during pregnancy can lead to birth complications that can affect your baby. Women who are over- or underweight should check with their OB or midwife to find out their recommended weight gain.

   2. Get those vitamins and minerals.

   - Without enough **iron**, important areas of your baby's brain won't grow as they should, and this could lead to permanent damage. Red meat, beans, fortified cereal, and spinach are wonderful sources of iron.
   - **Folic acid** is critical for the proper development of the neural tube. Eat some leafy green vegetables, such as kale and spinach. Dried beans and orange juice are also good sources. Fortunately, most breads, cereals, and grain products are fortified with extra folic acid.
   - There's new evidence linking adequate **calcium** intake to a decreased risk of severe toxemia—a pregnancy complication that can result in preterm delivery and improper fetal growth.
   - **Take your prenatal vitamins—even when you can't stomach the food!** It's often hard for a pregnant woman to take in all the nutrients she needs, especially during the first trimester of pregnancy, when the smell or taste of any food might send her to the toilet bowl rather than the kitchen table.

      The prenatal vitamins your doctor or midwife recommends are specially formulated for pregnancy. And before you ditch your vitamins because they make you sick, try taking them with food, or change brands.

Remember, prenatal vitamins are meant to supplement a well-balanced diet. They are not meant to replace the nutrients you need, merely add to them. Prenatal vitamins don't contain all the calcium and iron you need, for example.

3. Make sure you visit your dentist regularly. Women with gum disease are more likely than those with good gum health to deliver their babies prematurely. Some studies suggest that risk may be up to nine times higher! And being premature is not good for your baby girl's brain. Your natural incubator, your uterus, is better for her than any high tech machine in the neonatal intensive care unit.

4. Get your thyroid tested. Many women have an underactive thyroid gland that often goes undetected. A simple blood test can let you know whether you need to take a thyroid supplement, which can easily correct the problem. Children born to mothers with untreated thyroid disease during pregnancy score lower on IQ tests than children born to healthy moms.

5. Bump up your choline. The nutrient you never heard of is critical for your daughter's normal brain development. Studies in animals indicate that choline plays a crucial role in the construction of two major brain centers for learning and memory. A diet low in choline during pregnancy can permanently harm your baby girl's brain chemistry and development. Moms-to-be need 450 milligrams of the nutrient each day. That's easy if your diet includes eggs, beef, and dairy products. Soybeans are also a good source.

6. Eat fish, an excellent food, but certain fish can have high concentrations of mercury and should be avoided. Don't eat shark, swordfish, or king mackerel. Mercury can affect your daughter's brain development, and not in a good way. But fish, rich in omega-3 fatty acids, may boost your baby's brainpower.

7. Pump up the protein. Proteins are your girl's first set of building blocks. They help her grow from a single fertilized cell to a cuddly bundle. That's an awful lot of work for a little girl, and she needs your help.

● BABY GIRL BRAIN FACT ●
You Really Are What You Eat

So is your little girl. In a study from Harvard Medical School, the more fish women ate during the second trimester, the higher their babies scored on a mental development test at six months of age.

---

8. Stay away from alcohol. Alcohol is not good for developing babies. Alcohol passes directly through the placenta to your baby, and your baby's blood alcohol level will be about the same as yours. So if you're feeling tipsy, so is she. Alcohol can lead to brain damage. The most dangerous time seems to be during the mid second trimester, coinciding with rapid brain development, but no time is completely safe.

9. Give up the cigarettes while you're at it, and avoid illegal drugs. Babies whose mothers smoke are at even greater risk for being born prematurely. A smoking mother's placenta is smaller and doesn't work as well. Cigarette smoking actually raises testosterone levels in girl babies! Even worse, research indicates that girls born to smokers are four times more likely to take up smoking as adolescents, and to continue smoking, than girls whose mothers didn't smoke during pregnancy.

10. Get your body moving. It's good for you and may help boost your daughter's brainpower. There's evidence that at five years of age, children born to mothers who exercised while pregnant performed significantly better on general intelligence and oral language tests. The vibrations or sounds exercise causes *in utero* may have boosted neurological development. Not to mention exercise helps keep your weight gain under control!

● **BABY GIRL BRAIN FACT** ●

Mom's Stress

Maternal stress is passed on to fetuses. These stress chemicals can interfere with the production of brain neurons and synapses. There's some evidence that females exposed to stress *in utero* startle more easily and are more anxious than males. Ideally, a female fetus needs to find herself a happy, contented mom with a supportive spouse. That might not be realistic, however! We all have bad days, but if you are continually feeling overwhelmed by responsibilities, depressed, or angry, we recommend you seek help. It's OK to ask a professional for assistance for problems you can't resolve with the help of family or friends.

What Else Can I Do for My Baby's Brain?

Various authors and "experts" have suggested hyper-stimulating your baby at regular intervals to assist in her brain development. Suggestions include speaking to her through a paper tube, playing Mozart, reading to her in a foreign language, or shooting flashing lights at the mother's abdomen.

● **BABY GIRL BRAIN FACT** ●
The Role of Music

Listening to a soothing sonata is a great way to relax during pregnancy, but it won't make your baby any smarter. There is no evidence that playing classical CDs or foreign language tapes will boost your girl's brainpower, either before birth or after.

Does such stimulation work? There are numerous testimonials in advertisements supporting these methods. Users swear that their children are smarter, more physically coordinated and socially adept than average. Scientists, however, are skeptical. There is no way to really test how a baby would turn out with and without this stimulation.

No one can say for certain when a fetus is awake, so interfering with jabs to the abdomen may be interfering with your girl's natural sleep patterns. It seems counterintuitive to wake a sleeping newborn baby. Why would you do such a thing *in utero*?

Gently talking to your baby, however, seems to pose little risk, and in fact may help you as much as your baby. Thinking about your girl, talking to her, having your spouse talk to her, will all help to prepare you for this new girl who's going to jump into your life and turn it and herself upside down.

By now we hope you have a pretty good idea how genetics and hormones have combined to shape the baby girl in your womb or in your arms. Next, we'll give you a preview of what to expect this coming year and beyond, and what you and your husband can do to nurture the nature of this baby girl.

Her First Year

Your girl has arrived home, a stick-on bow attached to her head. Underneath that ribbon is a profoundly female brain that is about to make its presence known.

While you're exhausted with middle-of-the-night feedings, diaper changes, laundry, and just trying to find some time to brush your teeth, it seems as if all your little angel does is eat, sleep, and poop. Wondering how someone so small can demand so much of your time and attention, you might not notice that behind your daughter's seemingly simple existence an awe-inspiring process is taking place. Believe it or not, you're not the only one working hard!

You now know your daughter came home with a female brain. Her XX blueprint was created at the moment of conception. Without the testosterone hits received *in utero* by her male counterparts, her brain continued on the female default path, providing specialized circuitry for communication, emotional memory, and social connection.

As your daughter grows, her biological blueprint is directing her maturation process. Spurred on by signals from her brain, she will experience a "mini puberty," and her ovaries will produce estro-

---

● **BABY GIRL BRAIN FACT** ●
Faster Than a Speeding Bullet

In the first month of life, your daughter's brain will lay down three million neuron-to-neuron connections per second!

gen until she is two years old. Her basic wiring will be fine-tuned by her hormones and by experience. As your daughter responds to her environment—big brothers, the dog, your apartment, your backyard, whatever it might be—her brain will react by creating yet more circuitry, expanding on her girl wiring.

A girl brain shapes the way she sees, hears, smells, and tastes. Nerves run from her eyes, ears, nose, and tongue to her brain, and that brain will interpret all this data in a decidedly female fashion. Exactly how her brain structure affects who your daughter will become is the subject of continued dialogue. What is clear is that there *are* differences between girls and boys, and the gendered brain cannot be remolded. Your daughter will behave differently from her brother or her male cousin.

As an exhausted parent of a newborn, you may not be tuned into the many behavioral differences between your daughter and a newborn boy. At first, the early differences are obvious only to researchers. But if you had a previous child of a different sex or are the parents of boy-girl twins, those distinctions become increasingly apparent as you watch your babies grow.

What is clear to most fathers, however, is that many of his daughter's ways of experiencing the world are somewhat foreign to him. A daughter might seem like an alien creature to her dad, especially if that dad was raised in a house with brothers where sports and wrestling matches were the norm.

One of the gifts of parenting is how children have a way of challenging our assumptions. This can be true for mothers as well as fathers. Just because your daughter has an immature version of your anatomy, she may not be an immature version of you. Your daughter is about to open up new worlds for both of you.

If you ask most mothers, they'll tell you that boys are more active from the beginning, a fact Missy desperately wanted to refute as she raised her daughter Megan, age one, and her three-year-old son Andy. A former college soccer player and now a coach at the high school and collegiate level, Missy wanted to give her daughter all the opportunities for movement, exploration, and risk taking that she had given her son. Complaining at a practice to the mother of one of her soccer players, she said she just couldn't understand what was going on. Saying "no" to Andy's behavior was a momentary deterrent at best. She found her prohibitions at times actually spurred her son on. Although it was more work for her to get up and remove him from the situation, Missy secretly cheered on her boy's sense of adventure. Megan, however, was a completely different story. A gentle "no" or a raised eyebrow from Missy was enough not only to keep Megan away from the forbidden object, but it also frequently reduced her to inconsolable tears.

Missy was perceptive in noticing how different her daughter was from her son. Her two children did have something in common, however. They both began to experience and make sense of the world starting with their brains in sort of a physiological trickle-down effect that eventually worked its way to their feet.

What is going on inside that almost bald head you caress first thing each morning and (if you're lucky) only a few times during the

---

● BABY GIRL BRAIN FACT ●
You Say Po-tay-to and I Say Po-tah-to

Using PET scans and fMRIs, researchers have already detected one hundred structural differences between the female and male brain.

Baby Girl Story

Hannah is the mother of three, Cassidy and Laura, ages eighteen months and four years, and six-year-old Skyler. From early infancy Skyler couldn't have cared less about what Hannah dressed him in. As long as his diaper was dry and she kept the Cheerios coming, Skyler was content. The girls are another story. Theirs is a world of fairies, angels, and fantasized glamour. It's not breakfast cereal they lust after but pink princess gowns with matching shoes and anything that sparkles. Even the backpacks they carry to day care glitter.

night? This first year is a physical sensation roller coaster, both for you and your daughter. From the very beginning, your daughter is experiencing her world through all her senses—touch, sight, sound, smell, and taste—as a female person.

How Your Girl Experiences Sight

One of the first things your daughter's female brain will compel her to do is study faces. Whereas child developmental specialists originally thought all infants came wired for mutual gazing, your daughter may be more interested in staring at a human face than the newborn male. Most boys are just as happy to stare at a mobile wire sculpture.

At birth your daughter can see, but she can only focus on objects eight to twelve inches away and the object she wants to focus on is you. As parents, we respond to this deep, penetrating gaze. This back and forth dance, daughter to parent, parent to daughter, strengthens the neural connections that initiated the drama in the first place. Because your daughter responds so well to faces, chances are you'll be caught making a lot of faces at her. She'll get better at responding and she might mistake you for a clown. This interchange will reinforce her gazing activity as her brain assigns more and more neurons to support and hone her visual skill.

How Does Your Baby Girl See?

- By six weeks, she can focus at a distance of one to two feet.
- By four months, she can see objects, close or far, about as well as an adult.
- By six months, she'll see as well as she ever will.

Observers in the newborn nursery found that even at one day old, on average the girls preferred looking at live human faces while more boys were interested in looking at an object (the moving mobile over the bassinet). In fact, your daughter's skill in making eye contact increases 400 percent in the first three months of her life while a boy's interest in staring into his mother's eyes remains constant. By four months, your daughter will be able to distinguish pictures of people she knows from people she doesn't. Most boys can't do that at the same age!

How Does the Eye Work?

- Light traveling into the eye focuses at the back of the eyeball, on the retina.
- There are specialized cells in the retina, rods and cones, that detect light.
- The rods and cones are attached to nerves that collect together in the optic nerve. That nerve sends the information to the visual center of the brain.

Baby Girl Story

Jeremy was three years old when his mother, Paula, found out she was going to have a girl. Jeremy had been a delight from the day he was born. Curious and engaged, he was fascinated by everything—the ceiling fan, the music box with its rotating knob, and his parents. Paula approached her daughter's delivery with some ambivalence. She wondered how she would ever be able to love a second child as much as her Jeremy. But Ali amazed her. Her daughter studied every face that came near her, especially her mother's. She could hold on to everyone's gaze. Paula was taken aback by how quickly she fell in love with Ali. In fact, everyone did.

- Rods record a scene like a black-and-white TV set. They tell your girl the shape of things, and detect movement. They are very sensitive to light, and can "see" objects in very dim light (such as at nighttime), but not in color. Each human eye has about 120 million rods.

- Cones are responsible for color and fine detail. Each cone is sensitive to one of three colors—green, red, or blue. Cones only work in bright light, which is why you can't see colors at night. Each eye has about six million cones.

- Cells in the retina are primed to take in sex hormones, which means that eyes develop differently in girls and boys. Your daughter has more receptor rods and cones in her retina. With this surplus she's better able to take in the big picture. Your daughter may be better at seeing color and texture, but a male retina may be better at detecting motion. This was confirmed in a study of one-year-olds that found girls preferred films of people's faces but boys, even at this early age, preferred watching films of cars.

Helping Your Daughter Develop Sight

Make eye contact. Take advantage of those moments when your girl's eyes are open and focused on you. Look right into them. Each time she stares at you, she's building memory.

Respond to your daughter's glances. Your daughter takes meaning from every look. Little girls tend not to tolerate flat, expressionless faces.

Be an observer. Look for moments when your daughter is focusing on an object. Try not to distract her.

Let her reflect. Have your baby stare at herself in the mirror. At first, she may think she's just eyeing another cute kid, but she'll love making the "other" baby wave her arms and smile.

How Your Daughter Experiences Sound

Your girl has been listening to the muffled sounds of your world since the end of your second trimester. If Milo, your family dog, barked at the garbagemen, your daughter heard an *in utero* version of that barking. If her older brothers stormed into the house letting the back door slam behind them as they yelled across the kitchen, she heard that, too.

Once born, your daughter is able to demonstrate a superior ability at hearing and distinguishing sounds than most of her male counterparts. A female newborn can distinguish the cry of another baby from the general background noise, but boys in the nursery

● BABY GIRL BRAIN FACT ●
Your Newborn's Range of Hearing

In a study of 350 newborn baby girls and boys, researchers found that most girls can hear a broader range of sound frequency and tones in the human voice than can boys.

may not be able to do so. Baby girls respond twice as frequently to loud sounds as boys.

MRIs demonstrate that your daughter already uses more of her temporal lobe to hear than the boy next door. So it may be that the age-old parenting strategy of soothing a fussy girl by softly cooing and humming has its origins not in social stereotyping but in Mom's innate understanding of her daughter's biology.

How Does Your Baby Girl Hear?

- The outer ear, the part you can see and that you carefully bathe, collects sound and funnels it inward to the eardrum.
- When sound hits the eardrum, it causes three tiny bones in the middle ear to vibrate.
- These bones transfer their vibrations to the cochlea, the snail-shaped hearing organ in the inner ear. The cochlea is filled with fluid that moves with the vibrations. This stimulates tiny hairs in the cochlea.
- When the hair cells are stimulated, nerve impulses are generated that are sent along the auditory nerve to the temporal lobe, the part of the brain that is the hearing, speech, and memory center.

Baby Girl Story

Jane was worried, she confided to the nurse at her OB-GYN's office. She was back for her annual checkup. Her daughter, Lisa, was now eleven months old. Parenting had been a difficult adjustment for Jane and her husband, Rich. Lisa was the bright spot in their world.

Jane was amazed at Lisa's ability to detect the slightest tension in her voice. Rich and Jane began to disagree on a recent weekend trip. Just as Jane's throat tightened and her voice began to rise, Lisa started to cry. "It's frightening," Jane sighed. "What are we doing to her? We thought she was asleep!"

We have known for years that the majority of girls demonstrate superior hearing from birth on. Recently, technology has been able to give us a hint as to why this is. Girls are born with a shorter and more rigid cochlea. This difference makes a girl's hearing organ a more sensitive response mechanism than most boys of the same age.

● BABY GIRL BRAIN FACT ●
Her Heightened Hearing

When placed in a soundproof booth with high-quality equipment, scientists found that girls can hear much softer sounds than the faintest sounds audible to the boys. This difference is present as early as children can be reliably tested. They also found that when listening to natural language, females use both hemispheres of their brains, but males use primarily their left hemisphere.

Helping Your Girl Develop Hearing

Blab away. Your daughter needs you to react. Even though she is more skilled at hearing, she still needs your attention! When you're talking to her, leave short pauses where your girl would respond. Keep talking. She will catch on to your rhythm and will fill in the silent spaces.

Dads, modulate your voices! What may seem like normal banter to a father can be heard as a loud boom in your daughter's ears.

Activate her auditory wiring. Brain connections are built and strengthened when we use them. The more you repeat sounds, the more your girl's faint neural connections become fortified. Her auditory synapses will multiply steadily from nine months to two years.

Don't rely on TV and videos. Your daughter's brain learns best by interacting—hands-on, or in this case, "ears-on." Having music on in the background with you chattering in the fore is much more interactive than turning on an educational video.

How Your Girl Experiences Smell and Taste

Unlike your daughter's senses of sight and hearing, her sense of smell is fully developed at birth. In fact, smells will be one of her first experiences. It is the most developed of all her senses. The world smells and tastes differently to your daughter than it does to a newborn boy. Females detect more odors than males and when they do, they often react more strongly!

The smell and taste area in our brains is located in the limbic system, which is the seat of memory and emotions. We all remember the scent of something special like the lilac bushes in the backyard of our childhood home. This programming is quite powerful and begins at birth. Your daughter's nose plays an important role in her emotional development.

The nose is your daughter's main organ of taste as well as smell. The taste buds on her tongue can only distinguish four qualities—sweet, sour, bitter, and salty—all other tastes are detected by the smell receptors high up in her nasal passages. Your daughter has more discerning taste buds and she may prefer sweet tastes while baby boys may prefer the salty stuff.

Your daughter has been smelling and tasting throughout gestation. Inhaling and swallowing your amniotic fluid, her smelling receptors were bathed in sensation.

This sense of smell is extremely important in your daughter's life. Until she can see better, her world is what is in close proximity to her, and it is perceived best through her nose.

How Does Your Baby Girl's Sense of Smell Work?

- The smell sensor, the olfactory epithelium, is located up in the nose. In your nose it would be about three inches from your nostrils.

- Smells in the form of chemical molecules enter the nose, dissolve in the mucus, and stimulate cells in the smell sensors. These cells connect with the olfactory nerve, which sends nerve impulses to her brain.

- Your daughter has over forty million smell receptors in her nose.

- Although research tells us that newborns can respond within the first few hours of life to the smell of their mother's breast, this skill has actually only been observed in girls. When infant girls were given the choice of playing with a good-smelling rattle or a nonodorized one, they picked the scented one. Boys showed no preference.

Baby Girl Story

Sharon, a junior high teacher, observed that her infant daughter, Leslie, reacted far differently to a poopy diaper than her older brother did at the same age.

Leslie would crawl behind the dining room drapes to have a bowel movement. Sharon and Bill laughed as they heard Leslie's whimpers from behind the drapes. They both knew she wouldn't be happy until her diaper was changed. At the same age, her brother continued to play unperturbed until his parents tracked him down from the odor. Sharon joked that her nine-month-old daughter was more skilled at distinguishing what smelled good from what smelled stinky than either her brother or the average eighth-grade male student in her science class.

How Does Your Baby Girl's Sense of Taste Work?

In general girls have more taste buds than boys.

- Chemicals from food dissolve in saliva and bathe the taste buds on your daughter's tongue.
- Each taste bud has 50 to 150 receptors that respond best to one of the four basic tastes—sweet, salty, sour, and bitter.
- Just as with her sense of smell, nerve impulses go out to her brain, to the cerebral cortex and to the limbic system.
- Variations in a taste receptor gene influences taste sensitivity and explains why your daughter loves the peas but her brother spits them out.
- Seventy-five percent of what your daughter perceives as taste actually comes from her sense of smell. That's why, when your baby has a cold, she's not interested in food!

Helping Your Girl Develop Taste

Breast-feed, breast-feed, breast-feed. Yes, you're tired. It would be so nice to have your husband take over one night and let you sleep. But if you've never tasted breast milk, it really is yummy. Yes, there are drawbacks to breast-feeding (lack of sleep is probably coming to your mind at this moment!). We'd be remiss, however, if we did not note that research keeps uncovering reasons why breast milk remains the best. There are many wonderful books on infant nutrition and breast-feeding. These books discuss how some mothers deal with being on call 24/7 by pumping milk to be used in bottles given by Dad or a caregiver or by supplementing breast milk with formula. Ask your pediatrician to recommend a favorite book on infant nutrition.

Give your girl lots of variety. When it's time to introduce solid foods, remember food and its textures are a chance for exploration and discovery.

But what if you can't breast-feed? There are reasons you may find yourself unable to breast-feed. Perhaps you have a medical condition or are taking medicine that can be harmful to your infant. Perhaps your daughter is a gnawer rather than a sucker, and despite consultation with a lactation expert, breast-feeding has become a tense and agonizing experience for you and your child. Or perhaps you are an adopting parent.

Whatever the reason, our advice is to relax and go easy on yourself. There are excellent formulas available. Ask your pediatrician which might be best for your baby. A definite advantage to bottle-feeding is being able to share the mealtime responsibilities with your partner. And you'll be able to know exactly how much your baby is getting each time she chows down.

How Your Girl Experiences Touch

Skin is the largest organ of your girl's body. From birth, the least sensitive girl in the nursery is far more sensitive to physical sensations than the most sensitive male. Tests of tactile sensitivity in the hands and fingers produce such striking differences between girls and boys that the results don't even overlap. Girls are far more sensitive to pressure on every part of their bodies. From the outset, a girl may become more irritated and anxious with changes in temperature or a wet diaper. Your princess really may be bothered by the pea.

Baby Girl Story

Michelle couldn't get over the differences between her twins, Sophie and Martin. When Martin came home from day care, full of good cheer, Michelle would find his socks bunched up in the toes of his boots. "He was totally oblivious!" Sophie, however, would fuss if her clothes didn't feel right. Turtlenecks were the bane of her existence and she would shriek in dismay if her socks weren't put on just so. Michelle laughed saying her life became so much easier once she learned to buy socks without toe seams!

How Does Your Baby Girl's Sense of Touch Work?

- Touch sensors reside in the bottom layer of her skin, called the dermis.
- Your baby's skin has about twenty different kinds of sensors that send information through her spinal cord to her brain. The most common receptors are those detecting heat, cold, pain, and pressure.

• Your daughter has more pain receptors than any other kind. That's a good thing, because pain receptors protect her from harm. Before her brain registers the fact that she's just touched a hot stove, her brain stem makes sure that she pulls her hand away and she'll react much more quickly than the boy who touches the same stove.

Helping Keep Your Princess Comfy

Listen to her whimpers. Your girl is acutely aware of her physical surroundings and will let you know when she isn't comfortable.

Get touchy-feely. Keep a box of differently textured fabrics for your girl to play with.

Don't be afraid to roughhouse. Your girl can benefit from the stimulation that Dad provides her. Don't panic when your husband insists on throwing her up in the air. He'll catch her!

Massage her. Your daughter will appreciate a gentle massage. There are many books or classes to take to help you develop the skill to calm a distraught baby through touch.

How Does Your Girl Learn to Speak?

It really is true, as most parents will tell you, that once your girl starts talking it may be hard to get her to stop. Your experience may be very different from that of the parent of one of her male age mates. On average, girls achieve earlier maturation in nearly every dimension of verbal ability—verbal memory, fluency, and later on in spelling and grammar.

Your girl may start talking on average one to two months before a baby boy. She may use more words and speak in longer sentences sooner. For many of you, this may be the first time you actually observe real differences between your daughter's development and your friends' sons.

Genes really do play a role in verbal skills and the differences between girls and boys can be identified by researchers even before your daughter starts talking. As early as three months of age, there are observable differences. By midway next year, your girl may be using about ninety words, forty more than her male cousin did at the same age.

Baby Girl Story

Flora almost had an accident as she was driving eighteen-month-old Sally to day care. Her older daughters had fallen in love with musicals. The latest was Oklahoma. *They had the CD playing in their car every time they went on a drive. To the delight of her sisters and the amazement of her mother, without any prompting, Sally belted out from her car seat, "I'm just a girl that can't say no!"*

Girls and boys use their brains differently when it comes to language. Technology lets us take a peek into the working brain and allows us to see the difference. Research is just beginning to shed some real light on what is going on in female and male brains that sets the stage for these differences. There is a striking difference between how males and females use the hemispheres of their brains, particularly the left one. Boys rely heavily on their left hemisphere, but girls tend to share the load more equally between left and right.

When researchers measured the size of the *planum temporale,* a language area in both hemispheres of the male and female brains, they found that females devoted an equal amount of space in both hemispheres to language, but males tipped the scales to the left.

Had researchers peeked in on your girl's brain on her first day of life, they would have been able to observe differences between her brain circuitry and the circuitry belonging to the boy born in the birthing suite next door. In her brain center for language and

---

● **BABY GIRL BRAIN FACT** ●
Brain Language Circuitry

All the brain circuitry for language is ready and waiting at birth for your daughter to start communicating with you, but the wires haven't all been connected. By birth, her genes created a basic map for language acquisition. Your girl has more neurons than she'll need for language acquisition and by year's end she'll begin pruning away those she didn't use. Your baby girl has wiring to spare; at birth she had all the neural connections necessary to speak any language in the world.

For the first two years of her life, your daughter's dynamic brain will experience the world by listening to you. Neurons will fire. When sounds and patterns are repeated, those same neurons will fire again and again. This is how connections are strengthened. Every time you see a cow and chant "moo, moo" it sets the stage for the day when your daughter will drive by a farm, see a cow, and do her best bellowing imitation from her car seat. There's truth when neuroscientists quip, "The neurons that fire together, wire together."

hearing, your girl had 11 percent more neurons than a baby boy. Just after she was born her neurons were already responding to the excited speech around her in different areas of her brain than he did in his. Researchers find that, by three months, when your girl hears your voice, the electrical activity in her girl brain will be different from that of a three-month-old boy. She was born with a larger language area in the left hemisphere and had a head start on that side! So now she's working on wiring the right hemisphere of her brain. Ultimately, this assists in her processing verbal information on both sides of her brain.

Research shows that nerve impulses from the right ear are directed to the left side of the brain, and vice versa. In one experiment, researchers put earphones on male and female children and played sounds to either the right or left ear. Boys in the study responded better and retained more of what they heard in the right ear, but your bilateral brained girl would be equally capable of retaining the input from either side.

Other brain imaging studies show us that the language centers known as Broca's and Wernicke's areas are proportionately larger in females than in males. She has more neurons, denser packing, and longer dendrites. With all these differences, it's no wonder your girl on average may use more words every day than the boys in her preschool classroom.

As if all these brain differences don't provide enough biological support for your budding "Chatty Cathy," researchers have found that even though girls and boys follow similar and predictable patterns of growth and development both *in utero* and beyond, there are measurable differences in when the upper airways and oral motor pathways develop in girls versus boys. Again it is a girl's anatomy that gives her a head start.

Even though your daughter is primed for speech and communicating, you can still help her.

Talk to her. Chattering gives her practice in hearing and listening, skills that are linked to language. In a study following forty families for the first three years of their babies' lives, researchers found families that talked more ended up hearing more from their daughters later on.

Get in the habit of reading to your daughter over and over. Babies as young as eight months old can recognize sequences in stories read to them repeatedly. Make your daughter the hero of your stories.

Limit the negative. Babies who hear a lot of "no," "don't," and "stop" have poorer language skills than girls who were raised in a more verbally encouraging environment.

Sing a song. Learn as many baby tunes as you can. Make up your own verses. Use rhymes. Your girl loves repetition. Singing is an opportunity to use a lot of language unconsciously.

Limit the TV and video time. Babies learn words from people, not videos. Researchers find the babies who were taught a word face to face rather than while watching a video were better able to match the word with its object.

Your Little Girl in Motion

This first year your girl will learn how to move and use her body. Initially, her movements are simply the uncontrolled, reflexive movements she was born with. Over time, she'll learn to move her body parts voluntarily. It will be an amazing transformation to watch as your helpless pink bundle is transformed into a purposeful, even bossy, little girl, staring you down, as she cries out "Mine!" when she clutches the dirty cracker she found on the sidewalk in front of your house.

● **BABY GIRL BRAIN FACT** ●
Orderly Development

Most babies begin developing motor skills from the center of the body outward and from head to tail. Your daughter will learn to control her head and neck before maneuvering her arms. Then she'll learn to maneuver her arms before manipulating her fingers.

Even if girls are physically more mature than boys, boys are generally more muscular. Motor differences are evident from birth. Researchers support what the old wives had observed, "Boys develop motor skills more quickly than girls." As a result, boys often crawl and walk at an earlier age than girls. A Lamaze classmate's son may walk two weeks before your daughter. Of course, "early" is a relative term, particularly in your daughter's lifespan! Although achieving these developmental milestones is often a source of pride among parents, the differences are not really that significant.

How Does She Touch Her Nose?
It's not that simple!

The brain controls all of the body's voluntary movements. Your daughter's motor cortex, located in the rear part of her frontal lobe, is the brain area most involved in controlling your daughter's voluntary movements.

Your daughter's motor cortex receives pieces of information from other areas of her brain. She needs to know where her body is; she needs to remember she wants to touch her nose; and then she needs to develop an appropriate strategy for attaining her goal—moving her hand. Each of these tasks is directed from a different area of her brain. To deploy her body parts smoothly, she needs an internal control center that can precisely regulate the sequence and duration of her movements. That control center is the cerebellum.

Those larger muscles that enabled your classmate's son to crawl earlier may also help him to run faster, jump farther, and climb higher than your daughter. Researchers attribute his skill to a boy's larger muscles and to his stronger visual-spatial relation skills (something we'll address in greater detail next chapter).

Baby Girl Story

Molly and Zeb were born three days apart. Their mothers met at a La Leche meeting when the babies were just weeks old, and they became fast friends as they shared their decaffeinated lattes and compared parenting notes. It was only natural when they decided to celebrate the babies' first birthdays together. Zeb's mom made chocolate cake and two highchairs were pulled up to the table. Both families helped the one-year-olds blow out the candles. Within seconds, Zeb dove into his piece of chocolate cake, chocolate frosting covering his face and his corduroy coveralls. Molly plucked the candle off her piece of cake and carefully began to lick the frosting off the candle before tackling her cake with her spoon.

Your girl may, however, outpace him in other aspects of motor development, particularly in fine motor or hand manipulation skills. She'll find the crayon your older preschooler left on the floor, and to your surprise will grab it and turn it around in her hand as she examines it. Such fine motor control will, in the next few years, give her success in many of her preschool learning activities, such as using scissors and fastening buttons. The boys in her future may be able to leap tall buildings but it's your girl who may first grab her rattle, pick up the Cheerios, and tie the laces on her Tinkerbell tennis shoes.

The greater number of connections between the two hemispheres of your daughter's brain helps give her a head start when it comes to large muscle activities that require coordination rather than strength, such as skipping, hopping, and balancing on one foot. The differences between girls' motor coordination versus boys' strength will be played out in her playground preferences down the road. Your girl may not win most of the footraces but she may best most of the boys in a jump rope competition!

Most important, remember that your daughter will develop at her own pace. She may have been the first one to crawl in your playgroup. Then again, when the other girls are taking steps on two dainty feet, your girl might be the one who remains anchored to the ground on all fours. Even though there are differences in how development unfolds between the genders, there is also variation within each gender.

Right now, motor milestones are the most obvious measure for parents of what's going on inside their children's brains. It's the rare mom or dad who doesn't feel secretly proud or disappointed as they compare their daughter's future Olympic aspirations to the other babies in her age group.

Baby Girl Story

Eugene and Cheryl now have three grown girls. Cheryl's niece was about to have a second girl of her own. Cheryl wanted to give her some advice; instead she gave her two pieces of yarn, one yellow and one pink, and tied them together. Each had a tiny bell connected to the end. Attached was a note reminding her that even though her children were both female she shouldn't count on them being similar.

She then shared this story of her first two girls. Erin, Cheryl's firstborn, had, by fifteen months of age, a collection of shoes that rivaled her mother's. Pink ones, ruby slippers, shiny black ones, jellies, and flip flops with flowers attached. She also let her mother know in no uncertain terms which of her collection she wanted to wear each day. Cheryl saved all of Erin's shoes and pulled them out when second born Hannah was a toddler. Hannah would have nothing to do with any of them. In fact, she couldn't stand having anything on her feet at all. Cheryl didn't use any of the shoes and ended up having to cut the feet out of Hannah's sleepers. It was the only way she'd wear them.

Girl Play for Motor Development

Despite their inborn differences, is it possible to encourage your daughter's motor development? Check this out:

Babyproof. Allow your girl play that is safe and unrestricted. Encourage her by giving her space to move in and explore. Put her on the floor so she can work on getting up herself.

Make like a monkey. Movement, such as rocking and hanging her upside down, helps develop her balance mechanisms.

Accent the positive. Call your daughter to come to you or place a favorite toy just out of reach so that she crawls toward it. This will help her engage in these actions on her own. She doesn't want to hear "no" at every turn and will quickly cease her exploration if she senses your disapproval. Besides, you'll get tired of saying it!

Give her a variety of toys. She may need you to get on the floor and show her how to use them!

Practice makes perfect. Don't hold her all the time. Give her chances to use the skills she's working on.

Be patient, give her the time. Yes, it's easier and more efficient to carry your daughter in a pack than to wait for her to take two steps, but the more mileage you give those little feet, the more muscle memory she develops. If she could, she'd thank you for not rushing her along.

Hormones Already?

Experienced parents of girls often warn parents of newborn baby girls about the emotional rollercoaster that is puberty. But hormones (aka "horrormones") are already at work. It's not only during puberty that hormones play a big role in your daughter's life.

The latest research is exploring the role hormones are playing right now—during infancy—in your daughter's brain and body. Yes, your daughter's ovaries are producing estrogen as an infant and will continue to do so for about twenty-four months. Scientists believe these surges of estrogen are needed to help set the stage for your daughter's future reproductive life. In the meantime, that same estrogen is also playing a role in shaping what is going on in your daughter's brain. This estrogen bath further strengthens your daughter's ability to communicate, connect, and bond.

And estrogen isn't the only hormone working in that female brain. Serotonin and oxytocin are *neurohormones,* chemicals that pass information between neurons, and they are found at higher levels in girls' brains. The higher levels of serotonin will help your daughter calm down and are thought to be responsible for making her less irritable than the boys in the nursery. Oxytocin, a bonding neurohormone, helps contribute to your girl's early ability to perceive and respond to the emotional atmosphere in the room.

Baby Girl Story

Janet didn't know whether to laugh or cry. While loading groceries onto her kitchen shelf, a bracket slipped and cans, boxes, and canisters came tumbling down in one large crash. Elise, Janet's sixteen-month-old daughter, and Caleb, her three-year-old son, came toddling and running in when they heard the clatter. They found Janet on the floor amidst the disaster. Caleb sat down next to her and began to contentedly munch on the raisins that were scattered across the kitchen floor. He was oblivious to his mom and the surrounding disaster. Elise began to rub her mother's shoulder, kissing her "owies."

Your Daughter and Her Female Parts

Kaylee remembers when Miranda discovered her hands. She was lying in her bassinet next to where Kaylee sat for a rare reading break. Kaylee could see Miranda waving her hands randomly. Suddenly the hands stopped in midair, and Miranda began to move them deliberately and slowly. Then the hands grasped each other and Miranda began chortling with glee.

Body discovery is part of the joy of being a newborn baby. Eventually, your daughter will discover her vulva and clitoris. Just as Miranda felt joy at discovering and controlling her hands, your daughter will soon discover that touching her vulva feels good. As she gets older, you might find her rubbing herself against a table leg, or rhythmically bouncing against a favorite stuffed animal.

As a mom, you might be confused. Do I stop her? Don't I?

This isn't masturbation. It's exploration. And for some children, this behavior can be self-soothing, much like thumb-sucking. If she gets a little carried away, this might be a good time to teach her about what's appropriate to do in privacy, rather than for all the world to see.

Baby Girl Story

Betsy and Seth had moved to a new city far from family and friends with their seventeen-month-old daughter, Jill. They found Floy, an older woman with an in-home day care, to care for Jill. The relationship between the families grew and Floy became a grandmother figure for Jill. One evening, Floy went over to Betsy and Seth's home for dinner. Unfamiliar with whether or not the family said grace before a meal, Floy asked if there were any rules at the dinner table. Jill announced to Floy with great seriousness that she was not allowed to touch her vagina at the dinner table. She told Floy if she wanted to do that she'd have to go in Jill's room for privacy.

But if you happen to see her trying to put a toy in her vagina, that's a good time to intervene. Just like stuffing a pea up her nose, there are some places a toddler ought not to put things. Many worried moms have taken their daughter to the doctor because of a vaginal discharge, only to have the pediatrician present them with a reclaimed yellow Lego.

Some Words About Cleaning Her During Diaper Changes

Newborn baby girls usually have a swollen vulva and a white mucous discharge. It may even be tinged with a bit of blood. This generally lasts for a few days and is the result of the huge amount of estrogen Mom had in her bloodstream.

Moms have grown up being taught always to wipe from front to back after using the toilet. One would think the same advice makes sense when it comes to cleaning your daughter at diaper change time. We're told this will reduce the risk of your little girl getting a bladder or vaginal infection, by cutting down her exposure to bowel bacteria.

There's no evidence to support this, however. And there is no evidence to support a meticulous scrub of all the vulvar folds and creases. Wiping gently with a clean, warm wash cloth and patting dry should be sufficient to keep your sweetie clean.

A Few Final Words About Dads

Fathers and mothers interact differently with their daughters. Moms tend to coo and soothe their girls. Dads tend to roughhouse with their children, boys *and* girls.

The bonding and attachment that seems to come so naturally for a mom is often a more conscious effort for a dad. But your daughter will benefit from daddy time. Dad needs to remember that his voice will sound loud to a little girl. Remember, infant girls hear sound at twice the volume boys do. Don't be surprised if Dad's deep male voice startles her at times.

Your daughter needs Dad to pedal her little legs, hang her upside down, poke her, and in general, stimulate her with gross motor activities that will evoke belly laughs. Your daughter, a master at relationship nuance, is paying attention to both of you from the start.

Remember Missy and Megan? Megan is walking and exploring now. She is taking a leadership role. Not on the soccer field yet, but in instructing Missy regarding who gets which pretty pony and where to put them. Megan never lets her mom have the purple pony.

Missy's learning to be patient. In the next chapter we'll look into the future to see what's awaiting Missy and Megan. Missy's hoping to enroll Megan in her first soccer tots class. She figures that by that time, Megan will be telling the players on the field where to stand. Missy also anticipates she'll be buying purple socks to go with that first pair of cleats.

But there's more than clothing and physical activity for Missy and Megan, and for you and your girl. Read on as we give you a glimpse of what is to come and how you can support this woman-in-waiting.

Gazing into the Future: Toddler and Preschool Girls

If you are like most parents, you won't remember much of your girl's first year. The details of her first smile, first steps, and first words are fuzzy, lost in the blur of sleepless nights and busy, over-scheduled days. By the end of that first year, however, you will have figured out the feeding and diapering routines. You'll be coming up for air just in time to witness a magical transformation—your daughter changing from a short, chubby toddling baby to a leaner, taller, chattering woman under construction.

With your girl changing at breakneck speed, how will you keep up? This chapter will walk you or, more appropriately, run you though a review of girls' motor, language, cognitive, emotional, and social development during their toddler and preschool years. We'll

---

• BABY GIRL BRAIN FACT •
The Exuberant Brain

At birth, your daughter had all the neurons she'll ever need in her cerebral cortex. But these neurons weren't very well connected to one another. In the first two years of life, connections between nerve cells will sprout out in a massive burst. At times, your daughter will be making these connections at an astonishing rate of two million every second! That adds up to about a quadrillion connections in that little head of hers. No wonder researchers call this the "exuberant period" of neural development!

also give you a glimpse of what's to come, because in the prover-
bial blink of an eye, you will be taking a picture of her sporting a
new pink Tinkerbell backpack as she heads off for that first day of
elementary school.

But first a bit about what is going on inside that head of hers.

A Short Introduction to Toddler and Preschool Girl Brain Development

Although new cells are born every day in the rest of your daughter's
body, she came with most of the brain cells right where they were
supposed to be. Those that hadn't found their rightful place spent
the early part of last year migrating there, growing larger and more
powerful. But these neurons didn't yet know how to talk to each
other.

During the first few years of your daughter's life, she will work
overtime to produce connections (synapses) between her neurons.
If you think of her brain cells as the trunk of the tree, she is send-
ing out roots and branches, axons and dendrites that are the communication systems between brain cells. By two years of age, she
will have over a hundred trillion synapses, far more than she'll ever
need. By the time your girl is three her brain will be three-quarters
of its adult weight and any one of her neurons may have made up to
fifteen thousand connections.

Creating Connections

It's a tough world out there for synapse survival. In a classic example
of "use it or lose it," some of your daughter's neural connections will

be pruned away due to lack of use. Without a job description and a purpose, a synapse will wither away.

Nature will vigorously be cutting back the number of synapses by the time your daughter is in fourth or fifth grade. You don't have to worry, because this is a natural process. If you think back to that tree image, a gardener knows that to get the best blossoms some pruning needs to be done. Extra shoots are snipped away. Your daughter's brain is set up to do the same thing, leaving only those connections that are really necessary for her to respond efficiently. Without this pruning, your daughter wouldn't be able to walk or talk properly. In the end, she'll have a leaner, meaner, more efficiently functioning brain.

Your daughter's genetic blueprint is responsible for the basic wiring plan in her brain and the order in which she will mature. The environment you provide her is interacting every step of the way with that blueprint. Experience is responsible for fine-tuning those genetically determined connections, helping your daughter adapt to her particular environment (where you live or the fact that she's the second daughter in your family configuration). *Neural plasticity* is the term neuroscientists use to describe how your girl's brain organization is modified by experience.

As parents you can weigh in to a certain degree on what input those neurons will get, which of the paths will be stimulated, and which will be ignored. By providing your daughter with a variety of experiences—motor, sensory, and cognitive—you'll be giving more of her synapses a workout and a chance to survive the pruning shears.

We know you are bombarded with information about how to maximize the environment's effect on your daughter's wiring, especially from those ads guaranteeing a smarter girl, if only you would use their tapes or books or early learning curriculum. In reality, there is no special program you can buy that replaces what loving, responsive parenting will provide your daughter. You and your home are the ideal environment for her girl genes. Give your daughter ample opportunities to explore her world, keep her safe, and provide the security of your loving support. Have her listen to you sing and talk, send her outside to feel the wind and sun on her face, build sand castles at the beach, and she will have all the natural stimulation her brain needs.

Left Brain, Right Brain

For the first few years of your girl's life, the two hemispheres of her brain will develop at different rates. Your toddler's energy will be focused on growing that left hemisphere, the seat of language, logic, and mathematical skills. Your girl will experience a growth spurt in her left hemisphere earlier than her male counterpart. As her brain develops, your daughter will be taking on increasingly complex behaviors and will demonstrate leaps in her cognitive skills.

The white matter of your girl's developing brain is made up of the long arms of her neurons. These neurons help distribute information processing throughout her brain. One place in the brain where white matter is concentrated is the corpus callosum, a large bundle of fibers that links the two hemispheres of the brain. Some studies show that the shape, density, and size of your girl's corpus callosum are larger on average than her brother's was at this age. This heightened communication between the two hemispheres of her brain, researchers believe, gives your girl an advantage when it comes to relating to the world. She's more likely to multitask more constantly.

In elementary school her right hemisphere will step up to the developmental plate. Even though this won't happen for a while, her right hemisphere isn't being ignored. Later on in this chapter we'll talk more about how these brain differences affect both her behavior and her development.

● BABY GIRL BRAIN FACT ●
Fuel for Growth

The brainwork your baby girl is doing behind the scenes right now takes a lot of fuel, so during the first four years of her life she'll be using two times more glucose, the body's primary source of fuel, than you do. Her brain will be more than twice as active as yours, and it will remain so until she reaches puberty. Don't worry though! You don't have to run out to the pharmacy and buy a glucose supplement. Your girl will get all she needs from digesting the sugar and starch in your breast milk or her formula and from foods you are feeding her.

The Role of Myelin

Synapse creation isn't the only process happening inside your daughter's brain right now. Your angel may have come equipped with all her necessary brain cells, but there was very little myelin, a thick substance coating the length of her brain cells. Think insulation on an electrical cord.

Myelin helps your daughter's brain deliver messages from one cell to another more efficiently. With limited myelin, it takes your little one longer to do things than it will a few years from now. This is why your daughter takes a few moments to react when you request that she stop using her hairbrush on the kitty. The message needs to be heard, interpreted, and then the brush needs to be put down. That's a lot of information being fired and those connections don't react instantaneously yet. It takes a long time for the myelination process to reach completion. It starts now and will continue into her young adulthood. Your girl's brain will finish the myelination process several years ahead of that young man she will be dating.

These next few years will be the period of the most rapid myelination in her brain. The high percentage of fat in myelin (80 percent) is just one reason that fat intake should not be restricted during her first two years. Pediatricians recommend a diet that contains 50 percent of its calories from fat. Whole milk products are an excellent source of fat for her. After age two, however, fat intake should be limited to about 25–30 percent of calories.

Steps to Pirouettes—Your Little Girl in Motion

From that first time your daughter propelled herself precariously close to the edge of the bed, lunged on all fours toward her "stuffie," or toddled on unsteady feet toward your waiting arms, she has been gearing up to explore the world around her. All that internal energy and brain growth is being matched by an explosion of physical growth and activity as she manipulates objects, practices sounds, walks, hops, and then runs up and down stairs.

There will be days when your girl will be inexplicably fussy. Then a day or two later she'll start walking, or running, or she'll take on the stairs. All that fussiness is in preparation for that next bit of motor mastery. Your girl's world is expanding.

Her Gross Motor Skills

Gross motor activities, such as running, jumping, throwing, climbing, and kicking a ball, require skills that use the large muscles in your daughter's arms and legs. Advancements in these areas often appear to be so rapid that you might think she acquired these abilities overnight.

She's growing by leaps and bounds, too. By age two, your girl may be 50 percent of her adult height. She may reach this halfway point seven months (on average) before a toddler boy. She may also reach puberty earlier and stop growing much earlier. In the end, your girl may be first to the growth finish line but she won't always be the largest or the strongest.

Right now, however, she's working hard to keep pace with her male age mates. She'll hop better and move through space with more grace. She has a better sense of balance. The differences between your girl and her playground buddy are rooted within her genes and hormones. Women have only 55–58 percent of the upper body strength of men and on average are only 80 percent as strong as a man of identical weight.

The keen observer who spends any time on a playground or in a preschool classroom observing toddlers and preschoolers at play will see that girls and boys are using their bodies differently. By the age of three, differences emerge in the ability of females and males to throw a ball, with boys excelling in both distance and accuracy. Girls and boys differ in their jumping skills—girls are more precise in their jumps, but boys can leap higher.

In one study, preschool girls outperformed boys in four of six movements of a rhythmic ability test. Considering that rhythmic competence is strongly related to children's motor coordination, the

Baby Girl Story

Caitlin, age five, was three years younger than her sister, Elena. Both girls had started ballet lessons when they were two. Elena took to the classes and moved up to a more advanced level when she was five. She loved her hair bun, pink tights, and poufy tutu. The family living room was her ballet studio.

Caitlin, however, was just as happy playing soccer with the boys in their cul-de-sac as she was standing at the ballet barre. Concerned that she might be pushing her daughter to participate in something she didn't like, her mother asked her what she thought of ballet. Caitlin smiled and let her mom know it was just fine. She told her mom that standing on one leg in ballet helped her kick the soccer ball.

preschool girl can be encouraged to move to music. The sound you make with a wooden spoon on a pot just might inspire a cardio workout for your little one.

Her Gross Motor Skills at Play

Among preschoolers, girls spend 20 percent less time, or four hours less per week, in physical activities than boys do. Females underestimate their competency and skill when it comes to physical activity. Community preschool programs enroll more boys in sports programs than girls. In one community, a creative activity programmer changed the name of a sports program to Fun Stuff and Fitness. Registration for the program prior to the name change was 80 percent male and 20 percent female. After the name change, enrollment shifted. Girls now make up 53 percent of the Fun Stuff program.

Mothers might remember a moment when they no longer felt at ease joining the boys in their games of cops and robbers. Researchers found that by the age of six both boys and girls think that boys are better than girls at sports. It's important to share movement with your daughter starting now. We can't overemphasize the need for young girls to learn that they really are physically competent and that moving can be fun.

Motor development follows a specific course in toddlers and preschoolers, and it differs for girls and boys. These differences result from the hardwired sequencing pattern their brains follow. Once again the age-old adage that girls mature earlier than boys holds true. The neural systems that underlie motor development reach full maturity one year earlier for girls than for boys.

Your daughter's frontal lobes, the reasoning part of her brain, develop earlier and are more active than those of a boy her age. As a result, most girls are less impulsive in their play. Girls are able to organize and plan out a premeditated course of play complete with a complicated set of rules. This kind of play can look very different from the intimidating rough-and-tumble activities of the boys at your neighborhood playground. Difference in activity level and play preference are not necessarily deficits for either gender but a reflection of the toddler or preschooler's gendered brain.

The time it takes to reach maturity of the brain's motor control systems isn't the only difference between boys' and girls' roads to motor mastery. Researchers using fMRIs are looking at boys' and girls' developing brains as they perform the same task, such as throwing a ball. They are finding that boys and girls use different parts of the brain as they perform identical tasks.

Toddlers worldwide engage in goofy, silly play, which includes wrestling and chasing. These romps are often accompanied by laughter and screams. And as one father noted, his daughter and her friends could hit a range of high notes nearly capable of shattering their good crystal.

This wild play is useful for both your daughter's gross motor and social learning. Researchers believe this letting off of steam releases tension while exercising the large muscles in her arms and legs. Girls who may feel less skilled at organized sports may prefer the competition-free make-believe chase between daddy monster and Rosie on the run.

Baby Girl Story

Three-year-old Jasmine's preschool class was going to the pumpkin farm for a day that included apple and pumpkin picking and a hike in the autumn woods. The day was to end with a trek through a corn maze. Jasmine had been talking about the field trip for days. The night before the outing Jasmine carefully laid out her clothes for the next day; her pink straight skirt with the matching sweater and her shiny ruby slippers. Her mother, Tammy, tried to encourage her daughter to wear pants so she'd be free to play and move about. Tammy told her she'd have more fun playing. Tammy told her she'd be warmer. Jasmine held firm. Tammy tried the "You'll be able to run faster and be first to get through the corn maze" argument, to no avail. In exasperation, Tammy called up Jasmine's best friend's mother to find out what Lisa was wearing. When Jasmine heard Lisa was wearing her Dora the Explorer sweatshirt, she acquiesced and pulled out her pink sweats.

How to Help That Baby Girl Play Hard

Here's what you can do to help encourage your girl's physical play:

• *Make moving fun.* Reduce her performance anxiety by engaging her in noncompetitive physical activities.

• *Show her pictures* of skillful female athletes, and watch them perform.

• *Be one of those female role models.* Take her out on a bike trip, hike with her in the fairy forest, or go screaming with her as you jump off the dock into the freezing lake.

• *Pay attention to language and comments.* Your girl is fine-tuned to emotional nuance. She's quick to pick up on comments and attitudes from television, parents, and friends. Discourage such comments as "You throw like a girl."

• *Integrate activities.* Create fun games and crafts that include movement and action. Girls will take part in these activities without associating them with traditional sports.

• *Play blanket tug-of-war.* It will strengthen her arms and she'll love to cuddle up afterward.

• *Dance, dance, dance.*

Fine Motor Skills

Your daughter may have needed encouragement to jump off the sand dune on your family vacation at the beach. Chances are she won't need as much of your support or to hear "Good job!" quite so often when it comes to learning how to tie her shoes. The areas of her brain responsible for fine motor abilities are more fully developed in females during the toddler-preschool period of development.

During the next few years your daughter will be developing those fine motor skills: the tricky task of using her hands to effec-

Baby Girl Story

Susan had six-year-old twin boys, Alex and Ben, and a four-year-old daughter named Bev. She had never planned much for the twins' birthday parties. They lived on acreage and each party had pretty much been keeping the boys and their friends fed and watered while turning them loose outside. Bev's fourth birthday was coming up and Alex pulled his mother aside, suggesting she might want to plan something for the girls to do. Susan took his advice and made a food and snack scavenger hunt. The girls went traipsing through the property, giggling, dancing, and singing as they climbed trees and untied their bags of fruit, cookies, and juice hanging from the branches.

tively manipulate small objects. Those buttons, zippers, and snaps will be easier for her than they were for her brother. So will cutting with scissors or holding a paintbrush for the masterpieces that will adorn your refrigerator. Still, don't be in a hurry as she decides to take on one of these fine motor challenges. Her toddler "Me do!" mentality will take over and you'll have a battle on your hands if you try to hurry her out the door by doing the hooks on her shiny black Mary Janes for her!

There are ways to promote your daughter's fine motor development and continue to encourage her natural inclinations. Build fine motor practice into everyday activities:

• ***Have her join you in the kitchen.*** Let her frost cookies, spread peanut butter on bread, or cut up the bananas for the fruit salad. Her creations may not be ready for the food channel but she'll love serving the family and eating the end result.

- **Plant seeds in the garden.** Picking up bean seeds and putting them in the row requires a lot of skill. It's also a way to get your girl outside and learning about nature.
- **Open lids.** Enclose toys or snacks inside snap-top containers and let her take off the lid to get to the treat.
- **Eat your art.** Finger painting with pudding on wax paper is another fun way to develop those tiny movements and reward her tummy at the same time.
- **More food motivation.** Have her help you draw a Humpty Dumpty on an egg and then practice using gentle hands to crack that egg.

Your Baby Girl's Cognitive Development

How your daughter sees and perceives the world through all of her senses shapes how she will remember it. She will be using all her senses to interact with the world around her. She will be thinking, interpret-

● BABY GIRL BRAIN FACT ●
The Differences in Developing Cognitive Skills

By most measures of sensory and cognitive development, girls are more advanced in vision, hearing, memory, smell, and touch. In addition, in one large study, cognitive growth and social behavior were studied for over two thousand children between the ages of three and six-and-a-half (1,211 males and 1,207 females). In all age groups, females performed better than males in language and social skills.

ing, understanding, and forming memories of each of these experiences. Researchers call this cognitive development. These skills include information processing, language development, and memory. Your baby is now beginning to recall past events, imitate, imagine, and pretend.

A Word or Two About Attention-Deficit Disorder

Just as there is great overlap between how and when girls and boys develop cognitive skills, there is much variation within the two genders themselves. Although it's important to understand the different tendencies of each gender, not all children conform. When we begin to test children for their intellectual mastery we find more boys at the top and the bottom of the scale, with girls clustered in the middle. More boys than girls are diagnosed with learning disabilities such as dyslexia, delayed speech, and attention-deficit/hyperactivity disorder (ADHD). Boys with ADHD are easy to spot because they are frequently impulsive and disruptive.

Alarmingly, some studies estimate that as many as 50–75 percent of girls with ADHD are missed, as they are more likely only to have the attention problems without the hyperactivity. Often they are not disrupting the rest of the tots' music class, so it takes them longer to be identified and get the help they need.

Of course, there is the girl who is labeled "the tomboy." Preschool teachers and caregivers can easily locate her in the group. Even at a very young age, this girl stands out. She takes more risks than the other girls her age, playing roughly, throwing things, and finding herself unable to stop even when disciplined.

The tomboy, however, is not the typical girl with ADD. The shy, dreamy girl may also be diagnosed with ADD. She can easily

Baby Girl Story

John was worried about his daughter Serena. She seemed to be so out of it at times. The family joked about her blond hair, but it felt like more than that. His constant refrain of "pay attention" went unheeded. Sports had helped him focus when he was young, and so he registered Serena in the city parks and recreation soccer tots program. John was thrilled to see how excited she was about her new cleats and shin guards, but his pleasure was short-lived.

Observing the first practice from the sideline with the other parents, John saw Serena standing by herself at the opposite end of the soccer field, twisting and fidgeting with her hair. She seemed to have tuned out the coach and the other girls. Even when she participated, it appeared to John that his daughter was having difficulty following her coach's directions. Finally, a visit to their pediatrician confirmed his suspicion. She recommended Serena visit a children's therapist for an evaluation for ADD.

be overwhelmed by such things as too much noise or activity, or a caregiver's demands to do things a certain way. Boys with ADHD often react to these situations by acting out. This girl may retreat from the world. Just because a child is dreamy or shy, however, doesn't mean she has an attention-deficit disorder. This can just as easily be her temperament. As a parent of a shy girl, ask yourself, is my girl responding to a stressful situation? Is her behavior getting in her way?

Then too, there's also the girl with the hypersocial form of ADD. She is the nonstop talker. There's a difference between little Miss Congeniality and the girl who chatters constantly, overwhelming her play dates. She jumps from topic to topic and interrupts frequently. As a result, a girl with hypersocial ADD may find it hard to keep friends.

Your daughter may at times have trouble maintaining eye contact. She may yak your ear off. She may seem to be a space cadet. In each of these cases there's a difference between a girl whose temperament affects the way she interacts with the world and the girl who has a diagnosed disability. Perhaps a family member has made a comment or your day-care provider expressed her concern that your daughter is "struggling." Perhaps no one has said anything, but you are worried. Is there something wrong?

Preschools and day-care centers are not trained to make mental health diagnoses. Neither are family members. The only way to tell the difference between normal behavior and ADHD is with a thorough diagnostic assessment. If you are worried about your daughter, get an evaluation from a trained professional. Start with your pediatrician, but that may not be the last word. Ask for a referral to someone who specializes in working with attention disorders and girls. Most experts agree that there are ways to diagnose ADHD accurately, but they are also quick to point out that it may just be a matter of time before a girl grows up, gains courage and a sense of her self.

Focusing Behavior

All girls, no matter where they fall on the intellectual or behavioral spectrum, need help focusing and organizing their behavior. Studies show that girls don't fare as well as boys when it comes to short-term stress. It's a big and confusing world your girl is trying to navigate, so help her by providing her with

- Simple rules
- A reliable and consistent schedule
- Time outdoors, away from the world of electronic games and TV
- Ample "heads up" time when a transition is about to happen
- An organized room with designated places for her toys, clothes, and day-care supplies
- Your loving support and one-on-one time

Vision and Hearing

In a study where researchers looked at the electroencephalograms (EEGs) of five hundred boys and girls starting at two months of age, results showed that between birth and the age of six years, boys' and girls' brain development followed different trajectories. Your girl will develop certain skill sets before the boys in her age group and vice versa.

If from birth, your daughter was a visual and auditory kind of girl, she may notice things to which her male cousin is somewhat deaf and blind. She hears two to four times better than the average boy, which is one of the reasons why she backs off when you say "no" as she approaches the wrapped presents under your Christmas tree, and your nephew proceeds as if you hadn't said a thing. And when you go to hear the children's choir at church on Christmas Eve, chances are there'll be far more girl than boy members, because six times as many girls than boys can sing in tune. Your girl hears that tightening in your voice. She's more adept at noticing small changes

● BABY GIRL BRAIN FACT ●
Female Visual Discrimination

Girls and boys see some things differently and, as a result, what entertains them visually is different. When given a choice, girl toddlers will spend more time watching movies of faces than of vehicles. With more receptor cones and rods in her retina, girls are able to access a broader arc of visual data. Your daughter's heightened peripheral vision allows her to see the big picture.

in volume, which is why dads have that unique ability to get a tearful reaction out of their daughters just by verbally weighing in.

Spatial Reasoning

Spatial ability is perhaps the most frequently documented difference between boys and girls. Spatial skill allows your girl to accurately picture the shape, position, and proportion of objects in her mind's eye. There are literally hundreds of scientific studies documenting that boys excel in spatial reasoning.

Girls overcome many of these innate differences. In a study of three-year-olds, a group of girls and boys were given a set of tools to be used in maneuvering an out-of-reach object into arm's reach. Only one of the tools was capable of completing the task. Adults were available to offer helpful hints about which tool might work. After the children retrieved the first animal, they were given a duplicate set of tools to grab another. Seventy-seven percent of the boys were able to figure out on the first try which tool to use without adult help. Only 31 percent of the girls could do that. Once an adult explained to the girls how a tool worked, however, they were equally adept at manipulating it to retrieve both animals. Girls ultimately got to the same conclusion by using relationships with others, rather than spatial reasoning.

In general, research finds that girls stick with some tasks longer than boys and are better able to verbalize the strategy they used in solving a problem. Give your girl plenty of opportunity to build princess castles with blocks and assemble jigsaw puzzles. These activities will encourage the development of her spatial reasoning.

Touch

The male brain gives boys the edge in many areas, but your girl's female brain is organized to respond better to various sensory stimuli. Females are equipped to receive a wider range of sensory information and to connect and relate that information with greater facility. As her frontal lobes develop, she'll get better at interpreting sensory messages regarding danger and the need for self-control. She'll react faster to pain and will cry out more so she'll let you know when she accidentally touched a hot stove.

Despite her heightened sensory acuity, your girl will still overestimate her physical skill as she underestimates the fragility of that object on grandma's end table. Experienced parents can tell how old the daughter of the house is by how high up household treasures are stowed. Still on the coffee table? She isn't pulling herself up yet. Stored on the mantle? She's charging around the house with typical toddler abandon.

Language

Remember how your newborn daughter was intrigued by your face while the neighboring boy in the nursery was just as content to stare at the mobile hanging above his bassinet? The variation in their interest and fascination resulted from structural differences in their gendered brains. Testosterone *in utero* may account for those differences. It appears those fetal hits of testosterone affect how boys differ from girls in the development of language. We know that girls are exposed to less testosterone *in utero* than boys. According to some studies, infants exposed to lower levels of testosterone *in utero* (most girls) made more eye contact with the person holding them. And as a toddler they had more words in their vocabulary at different age milestones.

Without exposure to the male hits of testosterone *in utero,* your girl's brain is primed to acquire language at a rapid pace. The Broca's and Wernicke's areas of her brain develop sooner. Because these are the language centers of the brain, girls tend to develop better language skills and larger vocabularies ahead of their male counterparts. Just like a boy, your daughter processes words on one side of her brain, but unlike a boy she'll use both sides of her brain when deciphering sentences.

There is tremendous variability between when one toddler and another reaches language milestones. Language can develop continuously or it can arrive in a burst following a lengthy plateau. Like all children, your girl understands more than she expresses. Your daughter's first attempts at expressive language will in all likelihood be a series of nonsensical sounds that imitate the cadence and rhythm of your adult speech.

By the age of two, your girl may be turning into quite the conversationalist. She'll keep asking questions just to keep you talking. She'll tell you about what she has in her backpack, what she is wearing, what she ate for breakfast, what she likes, and what she doesn't. She's adding words to her vocabulary at lightning speed.

> ## • BABY GIRL BRAIN FACT •
> ### Her Greatest Pleasure
>
> Talking activates the pleasure centers in a girl's brain by releasing the neural chemicals dopamine and oxytocin. This is one of the biggest neurological rewards a girl can get.

Because girls talk earlier, your daughter may start her verbal practicing earlier. By the age of twenty months, your "Chatty Cathy" may have two to three times more words in her vocabulary than the boys in your mother-toddler play group. By the time she starts first grade she'll have fourteen thousand words to use as she tells you about her day. Boys will eventually catch up, but they may not get those words out with the same frequency or speed. He'll get 125 words out a minute to your speed queen's average of 250!

You can enhance your girl's developing language skills in the following ways:

• *Use props—books, puppets and pictures.* Choose books that show things you and your girl do, like playing with a dog or going to the zoo. Be sure to ask her lots of questions. Answering will give her a chance to use her growing vocabulary.

• *Keep up verbal stimuli.* Use your words to help her with math concepts. Talk about spatial relationships and opposites. Ask your daughter to give you directions. Ask your daughter, "Which one is bigger?"

• *Pay attention when your girl starts talking.* Attuned to the emotional climate, your girl will know when your mind wanders.

Autism—A Few Words for the Concerned Parent

It's no secret that autism affects boys more often than girls. Even though eighty percent of children diagnosed with autistic disorders are boys, girls are not immune.

Autism and other "pervasive developmental disorders" are medical conditions that are not caused by poor parenting. Although researchers are still looking for the causes of autism, there is growing evidence that genetics interacting with the environment *in utero* cause parts of the brain to develop differently in autistic children. Autism is not a form of mental retardation, but a difference in the way a child's social behavior, communication abilities, and internal interests develop. Some research is focusing on the role of intrauterine testosterone exposure. Children exposed to higher levels of testosterone *in utero* do have more difficulty making eye contact and developing friendships, and researchers are investigating whether very high levels of testosterone may contribute to the development of autism.

It's important to remember that each child achieves developmental milestones at her own pace. If you are worried about your daughter's language development, frequently a diagnostic red flag for autism, consult your pediatrician if your daughter is

- Not smiling at six months of age
- Not babbling, gesturing, or pointing by twelve months
- Not using single words by sixteen months of age and two-word sentences by two years
- Experiencing a loss in language or social skills

You are your daughter's advocate. Whenever you go to your pediatrician, go prepared. Have specific examples to discuss. It's OK to ask questions and to be persistent. If your physician uses terms you don't understand, ask for explanations. If you are feeling that your concerns have not been addressed or that you need more information, ask for a referral to a specialist such as a developmental pediatrician, psychologist, or a child psychiatrist. Remember, your pediatrician typically has about fifteen minutes to observe your daughter, but you have a wealth of data. Trust yourself.

Your Girl as a Social Being

Now that you daughter is moving and talking, she may exuberantly interact with the world and everyone in her vicinity. The brain that was drawn to gaze into the faces that surrounded her in the nursery is now being drawn to an even broader circle of people. Her perceptual skills are oriented to reading faces and inferring meaning to what she is seeing. During the next few years, you'll observe a leap in your daughter's social interactions with friends, both real and imaginary.

Baby Girl Story

Patty, the mother of three-year-old Liz and nine-month-old Holly, laughed as she recounted how Liz was already utilizing her negotiation skills when dealing with her feelings about her new sister. One morning when Patty was in the kitchen heating up some milk for Holly's baby cereal, Liz came up to her mother and told her she was worried about Holly. Patty stopped and asked what was wrong. Liz told her she thought Holly didn't need to eat today because she was getting chubby. She suggested that Patty shouldn't feed her. Then she proposed that Patty might have some time to read her a book as she didn't need to finish making Holly's cereal.

In a large study of preschool children, girls were found to be more socially competent than the boys in their peer group. The majority of girls, with their more mature brains, were better than boys at controlling their emotional reactions to conflict. As a result, they were less physically aggressive, less likely to express their anger outwardly, and less likely to use physical responses to resolve conflict. Verbally skilled and adept at reading expressions, they used negotiation for power, rather than physical aggression.

Your girl is learning how to make friends. She enjoys playing in small groups. She sees the big picture and attends to the needs of those in her circle. She is capable of taking turns. Even at this age, your girl has more oxytocin, sometimes referred to as "the love and cuddle hormone," coursing through her brain.

Not only will your girl have real friends, she'll share her world with imaginary ones as well. Don't worry. Imaginary friends are normal! Over two-thirds of all preschoolers have one. She'll discard her buddy as she does a toy when she outgrows it. The imaginary friend will go away, to be replaced by real ones who fill the same companionship need.

Friendship and Play

Friendships are very real to your daughter. Your girl will gravitate toward other girls. You'll see gender segregation in every preschool classroom. Most girls want to play with girls, and boys tend to play with other boys.

The rules are different for "girl" and "boy" play. Preserving harmony is frequently the focus of a girl's behavioral repertoire. When you eavesdrop in on your daughter's play date, you're likely to hear phrases like "Let's play" and "Whose turn is it?" If your girl is pushed around on the playground, she'll quit and find somewhere else to play. Your daughter will often be troubled by behaviors that don't even faze a boy, and when her feelings are hurt she may hold a grudge much longer than a boy will.

Girl play is about relationships and sharing. Researchers at Wellesley College found that three-year-old girls could interpret facial expressions as well as or better than the average five-year-old boy. A boy may want to build a taller tower and run faster than his best buddy. That's often not the case for your girl, who may focus more on relationships.

Gender Stereotypes or Normal Girl Behavior?

When asked what determines a girl or boy's toy choice, many parents answer "society's stereotypes." But monkeys are challenging that notion. It turns out monkeys' toy preferences are consistent with human gender choices. Though the monkeys have no concept of a "boy toy" or a "girl toy," male monkeys spend more time playing with cars and balls than female monkeys. The female monkeys spend more time playing with dolls than male monkeys. Presumably, monkey culture did not object to its daughters playing with cars and balls!

Developing Social Skills

You can help your girl fine-tune those social skills:

- **Provide your girl with lots of opportunities to play with peers.** There is no substitute for the real thing. Children especially benefit when they can develop long-lasting relationships.
- **Play with your girl like a peer just for the sake of having fun.** Your daughter will learn crucial skills through playing with other little people. But children also learn a great deal by playing

Baby Girl Story

Andrea, age four, was invited to her best friend Rena's birthday party. The girls first met at a mother-daughter co-op group and formed a close friendship from day one. Their mothers also shared a warm connection. When Becky took Andrea to the local children's store to buy Rena's present, Andrea said "no" to every gift her mother suggested. The only thing she wanted to buy Rena was a Barbie doll. Becky was horrified. She had vowed not to buy into the stereotypical toys that filled the aisles of toy stores. Andrea was inconsolable, crying "Barbie, Barbie, Barbie" to anyone within earshot. Becky acquiesced. At the party, she mouthed, "I'm sorry" to Rena's mom as Rena squealed with delight upon opening her gift.

with their parents. Laugh and smile often. Avoid criticizing. Be responsive to her ideas. Let her be the boss of play.

- ***Intervene when necessary.*** When she is playing with her best friend, let her work out her problems whenever possible.

- ***Keep an eye on the clock.*** Timing is everything for little ones. If your daughter missed a nap, you might consider canceling the play date. None of us are at our best when exhausted.

Early Discipline

As your daughter becomes more independent, she'll want to exercise more and more control over her environment. She wants to be in charge, and don't be surprised when the phrase, "You're not the boss of me!" comes spewing forth from your angel's mouth. As the parent of a toddler girl, you'll be asked to expand your discipline repertoire.

There are many reasons why you'll find it hard to discipline your daughter during the next few years. She's curious. She's bossy. She wants to say more than she's capable of. She's trying to make herself understood and it's a frustrating experience for both of you when she can't. Explaining that she can't do something won't stop your girl. You cannot reason with a toddler!

We promise things will change. Using MRI scans, researchers found that the area of the brain responsible for controlling aggression and impulsive behavior is larger in the female brain than in the male one. Give her time. She's still working on growing that mature brain.

Tantrums and Frustration

During the next year your daughter will probably have her first full-blown temper tantrum. You have done nothing wrong and in fact girls will give up their "tantruming" ways sooner than most boys.

Baby Girl Story

Mary, the mother of three-year-old Jana and seven-year-old Shelby, went on her first overnight business trip since Jana's birth. She called in the evening before the girls went to bed and was home on the next evening's flight. She stopped in the airport mall and bought each girl a headband with two floppy ball antennas attached by springs. She slipped a pair on and came bounding into the living room ready to hug her girls. Shelby took one look at her mom and burst out laughing. Jana burst into tears and hid behind her big sister. Mary took off the headband and went to console her daughter to no avail. Shelby, the wise elder sister, reminded her mother, "It's too late, Mommy. Those things are already running around inside Jana's body."

Her circuitry is just overloaded. She's trying to do too much, say too much, and master too much, and when she can't achieve her desired outcome, she'll get frustrated. This is normal. Once the tantrum is in motion, keep your girl safe and be calm. Her brain is trying to reestablish its equilibrium.

When angry, the male brain's amygdala releases adrenaline and sets in motion the "fight or flight" response. In the female brain, anger activates the hypothalamus. The hypothalamus controls digestion, among other things. Don't be surprised if, after a tantrum, your girl complains of a tummy ache.

Your daughter is trying to learn how to solve problems and deal with frustration. When researchers set up an obstacle wall and put a toddler on one side and his or her mother on the other, they were able to observe how girls and boys deal with their frustration. Eventually all the toddlers wanted to get to their mother and they would run into the obstacle. When confronted with this dilemma, the majority of girls didn't try to climb or push the obstacle down like the boys did. Girls cried out, attempting to engage Mom in the solution. For your daughter, relationship will be part of her solution toolbox.

Toilet Training

Although it actually is a brief period in a parent's life, toilet training may seem to stretch on forever. The good news is that girls, on average, express an interest in toilet training earlier, take less time to train, and are usually trained earlier than the typical boy. People will be full of advice as to how to approach this developmental milestone. Do I buy a separate potty chair or steps with a seat on our toilet? Do I use pull-up diapers or big girl panties? Ultimately, it's your call.

Take advantage of your daughter's skills at observing the world around her. Watching you use the bathroom will begin her toilet training. Put the potty chair where she can get to it when she is playing. Have her sit on it periodically. Keep an eye out for the physical signals; holding her vagina, jumping up and down, or pushing her knees together. Make sure she has clothes that she can get into and out of on her own, or let her run around without any clothes at all. That will help her get to the potty quickly!

Your baby girl will make mistakes, but she'll catch on. Celebrate her success with big girl panties. Your girl will need to learn to wipe herself properly, front to back. If she's having difficulty remembering which direction to wipe, have her pat herself dry instead.

Baby Girl Story

Four-year-old Emily came home from preschool with a question. "Mommy, do I have bad aim?" Her mother, Ally, explained that she thought Emily was really pretty good at getting the basketball in the basket and she even got close when playing pin the tail on the donkey. She asked Emily why she was worried about her aim. Emily explained that Mrs. Jones had come out of the bathroom at school that day and said that someone in their class didn't have good aim.

Sometimes girls will get a bladder infection when they are toilet training. If your daughter complains about pain when she urinates or is urinating more frequently than usual, ask your pediatrician about potential infection.

If your daughter has an older brother, or if she goes to a day-care center with mostly boys in her age group, she may want to try standing up to pee. It won't take but a couple of times for her to figure out that standing up won't work for her. If she persists, have her watch mom and tell her that is the special way moms and their girls go to the bathroom.

Gender Stabilization

By the age of two-and-a-half, your daughter will develop a curiosity about and an awareness of gender differences. She discovers there are two kinds of bodies, hers and the other kind. She pokes and prods her body. At times, to her parents' dismay, she'll want to explore her vagina or any other hole she encounters.

Girls will want to imitate their mothers or older sisters. During her toddler-preschool years, your daughter will develop a clear-cut sense of the fact she is a girl. She'll be conscious that girls have vaginas and boys have penises. She may still think it's possible that her sex might change someday. The tantrum she has when you take her for her first haircut may be the result of her fear that she'll become a boy if her hair is too short!

Are you getting tired of froofroo? Your toddler-preschooler can be very "girly," insisting on pink clothes, princess shoes, and tiaras. During this time your girl may engage in what you might consider "extreme stereotypical" behavior as she formulates her definition of herself as a woman-to-be. Many parents try to raise their girls without stereotypes. They buy gender-neutral clothes and have athletic equipment and blocks in their girls' playrooms. Despite these

Baby Girl Story

Melissa would jokingly wonder aloud if four-year-old Anneka really was her daughter. Their styles, interests, and choices in clothing couldn't have been more different. Melissa wore clothing for comfort. Anneka dressed as if the fashion paparazzi were around the next corner about to take her picture. Each day Melissa would drive the nursery school carpool past the neighborhood elementary school. The boys in the carpool would invariably get involved in descriptions of the bus and a discussion on how engines work. Not her Anneka! Today it was the girl getting on the bus with the leopard spotted coat and red backpack that caught her eye. Anneka was becoming a regular fashion diva, much to her mother's chagrin.

efforts, girls may make a family of trucks with a papa, mama, and baby in the garage.

You might be feeling like a failure, as your daughter wants to play exclusively with her dollies. You won't be able to discourage her interests, because they have been part of her wiring since her days *in utero*. She's having fun! This period, which child psychologists call "gender stabilization," may last through her preschool years. By the age of five, your girl will realize she won't become a boy after all. Then you might have a chance of going to the hairdresser without that tantrum.

Child Care, Preschool, and Beyond

Perhaps you'll be returning to work in the next few months. Perhaps you'll want your girl to have more opportunities to socialize with other children her own age. Perhaps your daughter's first academic experience will be in kindergarten. In any case, your girl will, within the next few years, find herself in a school-like setting. As the parent of a girl, you'll need to be an advocate for her and the female brain that will accompany her to school.

Children have less difficulty when they start school at a time when they are developmentally mature enough to handle the demands of the classroom. In reality the school setting is a good fit for most girls. Most programs emphasize verbal activities, arts, and social interactions, areas where most girls excel. Studies of early childhood learning settings indicate that girls have 50 percent fewer referrals to specialists for communication and speech delays.

Given their superior language skills, girls like learning through narrative. Give them a song to learn and girls want to know who wrote the song and where it was written. Boys are just as happy playing the percussion accompaniment.

Girls explore less and cause fewer discipline problems for their teachers and caregivers. As a result, half as many girls experience discipline difficulties in kindergarten as boys.

● BABY GIRL BRAIN FACT ●
Mom's Reassurance

In one study of toddler behavior, researchers sent toddlers into a playroom with their mothers. The researcher instructed the toddler not to touch a specific object in the room. Girls looked at their mothers ten to twenty times more than boys in the study, and did not touch the object. Boys went ahead and touched the object.

Accommodating Girl Style

There has been much written in the popular media about how girls and boys are underserved in different ways by educational institutions. In a recent study of how boys and girls rate their intellectual skills, researchers found that boys rate themselves higher than test scores measure. Girls, however, rate themselves lower than their scores indicate.

We know girls and boys learn differently. They use different areas of their brains to accomplish the same task. The physical location of a lesson may be important to a boy, but not to a girl. What is important to your girl may be whom she works with or sits next to. Competition, such as skills relays, may make her nervous. Girls may chatter to themselves wherever they are, talking their way through a lesson, and they may naturally break up in groups of three and four to work on problems.

When finding a child-care setting or preschool for your girl, it's important to take the unique learning needs of a girl into consideration. Make sure there are opportunities for

• *A girl-friendly space* that is safe, comfortable, and welcoming. Forget hard plastic chairs. She wants comfortable beanbags. Soft music and lighting will soothe her.

• *Risk-taking play.* Your girl doesn't need to be sitting still all the time to be learning the skills necessary for elementary school and beyond. Pushing her physical limits will build her self-confidence. One creative kindergarten educator created what she calls "dare training" for her five-year-old girls. She puts mattresses on the floor, and "dares" the girls to jump from a table onto the mattress. She also encourages the girls to yell as loud as they can as they do their jump.

• *Hands-on learning.* Girls learn in many ways. Giving her opportunities to touch, move, climb, and build things will help her develop her spatial relation skills.

Variety Among Girls

Just as there is variation between the genders, there is tremendous variation within gender. There are many different kinds of girls. They are girls who are highly feminine and chatty and girls who are physically competitive. There is the girl artist who is just as happy completing an art project as she is playing in the housekeeping area of her playroom. Not all girls turn inanimate objects into surrogate babies. There is no average girl. Parenting your daughter will be an adventure in getting to know who she is.

Lynne, the mother of three daughters, will attest to that. This past year, her husband's company relocated and the family would be moving across the country. When Lynne and her husband sat the girls down to tell them about the move, their reactions couldn't have been more different. Lizzie, age ten, burst into tears; Logan, age eight, grabbed her basketball and went outside to shoot hoops, saying, "You guys do what you have to do"; Cass, age five, started singing, "Make new friends but keep the old." Lynne wasn't surprised at all.

By now, you are beginning to feel more comfortable parenting whoever your daughter is. You've likely discovered that mothers and fathers parent differently, based on their own gendered brains. One thing is for sure. You both love your daughter without reservation. You both would readily risk danger to protect her.

In the next chapter we'll talk about the biological differences in mommy and daddy brains and how it affects the way you both parent. We'll look at resources available to support both of you and offer some final tips as you forge forward in your on-the-job-training of raising a daughter.

A Baby Girl Is
a Family Affair!
Circles of Support

Larry is a psychiatrist and the father of two daughters and a son. He once confided to a friend, "We don't have children to feel better, we have children to feel more."

Larry is right, but you don't have to travel alone on this exhilarating, yet often overwhelming journey of feelings. There is much wisdom out there for the newly born parent. It comes from the scientific community and the research we have reviewed; from educators who have spent tens of thousands of hours observing children and their behavior; from professionals in your community; from your family, spouse or partner, and the parents in your friendship circle.

The advice will vary, because mothers and fathers do parent differently. Just as your daughter's personality unfolds based on her female gender, the differences in parenting between you and your spouse are also the result of biology interfacing with experience. How we respond as mothers and fathers is linked to our own gendered brains.

Carl Whitaker, a noted family therapist, describes the differing roles of mothers and fathers by using a tire analogy as a metaphor for the family. If one thinks of the children in the family as the spokes on the wheel, the mother with her female brain is primed for attachment and relationship. She functions as the hub of the wheel, keeping the spokes connected at the center. The father, biologically programmed for risk taking and exploration, functions as the rim, experiencing the external world and the bumps in the road along the way. He protects the spokes and hub. Your spoke, your daughter, needs both a hub and a rim as she travels the road of her life.

Baby Girl Story

Sophie and David were shopping at the grocery store with their three-year-old twin girls, Naomi and Judith, when Sophie started to panic. She couldn't see the twins. They were chasing each other throughout the store and exploring the contents of the shelves several aisles away. David dismissed Sophie's concern as that of an overprotective mother. Sophie shot back, "My umbilical cord is only so long!" With a brain wired for attachment, Sophie wanted to pull them closer. With a brain wired for protection and action, David just had to get them back in sight. The testosterone coursing through David's body allowed him to feel more comfortable with his girls' exploration of the store, and within two minutes he had found them in the produce section.

The Biology of Mother and Father Brains

While your daughter began growing her female brain *in utero,* you, her parents, were each growing a mother or father brain. Advances in research not only demonstrate the differences between the male and female brains but also the difference between a maternal and a nonmaternal brain. The dramatic hormonal fluctuations that occur during pregnancy, birth, and lactation are in part responsible for remodeling the female brain.

Pregnancy and motherhood change the structure of the female mammal's brain, making mothers attentive to their young and better equipped to care for them. Brain pathways that handle the stressors of a child-free existence require less efficiency, resiliency and resourcefulness than the brain of a sleep-deprived mother attempting to juggle work, laundry, a diaper bag, a car seat, and a fussy baby girl.

The brain continues to develop throughout the human life span. New pathways form in response to new challenges and experiences. Before becoming a parent, how many of us have had the experience of trying to calm a screaming baby while driving fifty-five miles an hour and listening to the latest world news crisis, in an attempt to arrive at the sitter's with enough time to get to work by 8:30 A.M.? A brain researcher describes the drama of becoming a parent as a "revolution for the brain."

A Mother's Response

New research indicates that the hormonal fluctuations during pregnancy permanently alter the neural pathways in a mother's brain. Women frequently come into their OB visits asking questions not only about their bodies but about their brains.

"I'm scattered. I forget things all the time. Will I get my brain back?"

The diagnosis is "Pregmentia," we joke. But in fact the pregnant woman and her developing mother brain are undergoing some startling changes.

In a Canadian study, researchers took blood samples from thirty-four couples at different times during pregnancy and shortly after birth. They monitored the levels of oxytocin, cortisol, and prolactin in both men and women.

Oxytocin is one of nature's chief tools for creating a mother. The number of oxytocin receptors in the expectant mother's brain multiplies dramatically near the end of her pregnancy. This makes for a more responsive mother. Mothers continue producing oxytocin as a result of breast-feeding and holding their babies. Babies who are responded to are more responsive, and this makes moms respond more readily, thus setting a positive feedback loop in motion. With

✳ Mommy Brain Story

Amy came into her therapist's office in tears. Before giving birth to her daughter she was a high-powered manager in a large software company. She and her husband had decided for the first few years of their daughter's life that she would stay home as a full-time parent. In a blink of an eye, she had become the mommy who forgot things all the time, who got frustrated at little things, and who didn't work in a big office building in the city like Daddy.

She was worried about the kind of role model she was providing her daughter. Her daughter didn't see her as the woman who had a master's degree, who formerly managed million-dollar accounts. Amy knew that she had been the smartest girl in elementary school, but now she was afraid her daughter was coming to the conclusion that Mommy might not be too smart.

Her therapist told her not to worry. Amy's brain was fine, just adapting to its new role. Her daughter's perception of her would be fine as well, her therapist added.

---

oxytocin levels elevated, new mothers' brains are producing new synapses, creating the hardwiring necessary for maternal behaviors.

Released in response to signals from the amygdala, cortisol is a stress hormone that is also an important indicator of attachment. Mothers with higher cortisol levels can detect their baby's smell more readily than mothers with lower levels. These mothers also describe feeling a greater closeness with their babies.

Prolactin, the hormone responsible for lactation, was the last hormone studied. Babies by their very nature give us the opportunity to have our brain altered. Your girl's demands that you hold

Mommy Brain Fact   *Under the Influence*
An interesting side effect of maternal oxytocin surges is that moms not only bond with their babies, but with any male who happens to be around. A good reason for dads to be available during this time!

her and feed her multiple times during the day and night result in higher prolactin levels. And when the brain is exposed to prolactin for long periods of time, the opioid system is stimulated. Family bonding can be a real high for the new mother!

With all these hormonal influences at work, women are primed for the style of nurturance associated with "mothering." The oxytocin that is coursing through her body is likely to heighten her awareness of her baby and her needs. In most cases it's Mom for whom a toddler calls out when she gets an "owie," and most mothers will respond with expressions of direct empathy.

New mothers are more likely to relinquish their personal time and independence in order to care for their new infants. It is quite common for a mother to struggle with maintaining so-called "selfish" activities, such as personal hygiene and exercise, during the early months of her daughter's life.

A Father's Response

But Mom is not the only one experiencing hormonal upheaval during pregnancy and the early days of parenting! In the same Canadian research studies that examined mothers' levels of oxytocin, prolactin, and cortisol, researchers suggested that there is much more to masculinity than testosterone. Although testosterone is certainly important in driving men to conceive a child, it takes a collection of other hormones to make a father.

In a study published in the *Mayo Clinic Proceedings,* researchers found that new fathers have higher levels of estrogen, the hormone typically associated with women. During pregnancy and the postpartum period, men go through a hormonal shift just as their partners do. Surprisingly, 90 percent of men report experiencing occasional physical symptoms such as nausea and weight gain during their wife's pregnancy. It turns out that nature may play a role in preparing men as well as women to be committed parents.

These studies also found that fathers' prolactin and cortisol levels were in flux. In the three weeks before a child's birth, fathers' prolactin levels went up approximately 20 percent, and cortisol levels were two times greater during this period than during early pregnancy.

Although present and active during bonding in the mother and infant, vasopressin plays a much bigger role in the new father's neural chemistry. Vasopressin, a hormone synthesized in the hypothalamus and stored in the pituitary gland, is known to influence pair bonding. Vasopressin is released in the male in response to nearness and touch. When Daddy is at home during those first few days, vasopressin is released at high levels and helps him bond with his new daughter.

Daddy Brain Fact   *Dads Have Hormones Too!*
For the first month of a newborn's life, her father's testosterone levels decrease as much as 33 percent. Don't worry, Dads. Testosterone will return to its pre-pregnancy levels. One psychologist suggests that the decline is responsible for helping a father bond with his daughter and allows for the nurturing aspects of Dad's personality to be present during the first few weeks of his daughter's life

❋ Daddy Brain Story

Scott was going to stay home alone with the baby for the first time since her birth. Kirsty was off to the grocery store for just a few items, and she was nervous, as she wasn't supplementing her breast milk with any bottles. She began to provide Scott with a litany of things he could and should do for their baby in her absence. Finally, in exasperation, Scott looked at her and exclaimed, "Kirsty, I may not have breasts but I do have a brain!"

Following those first early weeks of parenting, a father's testosterone levels will reassert themselves at previous levels, and his male brain wiring will set the stage for a father's unique style of nurturance.

Fathers have a more physical, rough-and-tumble relationship with their children. A father's spatial and mechanical skills provide a different set of learning opportunities for a girl's interaction with the world. A father is more likely to lift his daughter in the air, hugging her and moving her around carefully but more rapidly than Mom. And as your daughter gets older, Dad may be the one throwing balls, wrestling, and teaching her how to play darts, encouraging your daughter's female brain to develop different synapses.

A father's parenting interactions may come more in short, active bursts rather than the ongoing, hands-on parenting that a mother provides. Dad will get in there and stir things up with his energy just when Mom thinks things have settled down. He'll set up competitive obstacle courses in the living room, through the hall, and out into the kitchen. He'll encourage his child to push her physical limits, often to Mom's dismay.

A MOTHER AND FATHER BRAIN STORY

Anna and Tim had invited their best friends over for dinner and a movie. Anna had just finished nursing Cleo when Tim picked her up and started flying her through the air. Anna kept telling Tim to stop, reminding him that Cleo was full and she'd probably throw up. In one final flourish, Tim flew Cleo high over his head and opened his mouth, saying a big "Ahhhhh" just as Cleo decided to release the contents of her stomach in his mouth.

Mom and Dad Under One Roof

As mothers and fathers express their gendered brain through parenting, stylistic differences become inevitable. If conflicts haven't come up yet between you and your spouse, don't be surprised when they do.

Fathers think that mothers worry too much about their children. Mothers, responding to their own biology, parent with an emotional range far greater than that of their husbands. As moms and dads play with their children on the backyard swing set, Mom is more likely to worry about her baby's safety as Dad pushes both his daughter's limits and the swing higher and higher.

As their daughter yells out, "Look at me!" moms will likely say something along the lines of, "Be careful! Don't go too high!" But dads may encourage their girl to see just how high she can swing. And then if the inevitable happens and she falls from the swing, Dad may think that Mom is being too soft as she comforts her girl and kisses her "boo-boo."

Loaded with estrogen and oxytocin, mothers are primed for the maternal instinct that parenting a newborn requires. The majority of

---

A MOTHER AND FATHER BRAIN STORY

Maggie and Lloyd took their girls, ages two and five, up to the mountain for a cross-country skiing weekend. After skiing with the two-year-old on their backs for most of the day, the parents returned to the lodge. Emma was squirmy and needed an opportunity to run around. Lloyd grabbed a sled and was about to take Emma up a small hill when Maggie yelled after him about how icy the hill was. Lloyd wasn't worried. At that precise moment, Emma came flying off the sled face down. By the time Maggie caught up to her, she was sitting up with blood dripping from the scrapes on her face. Maggie was furious. Before she could intervene however, Lloyd had scooped Emma up, ready for another run.

---

mothers win the gold medal when it comes to nurturing behaviors such as feeding, diapering, and caring for an ill child. And when asked, mothers say they like performing these caring duties more than their husbands do.

Just as your daughter may use more words than her male counterparts, mothers continue the pattern, using more words when talking to her girl than Dad will. Fathers want the facts and mothers want to talk about how their daughter feels about the facts. She'll encourage her daughter to "use her words" when processing a problem, but Dad is more likely to tell her to "shake it off." That same father may set up a race between his daughters. When one of the sisters wins and the other bursts into tears of disappointment and frustration, there may be fewer cuddles and words of solace from Dad. But Mom may be right there comforting the loser and asking her what Mom could do to make it all better.

Given moms' greater interest and desire to perform the "basics" of early parenting, they tend to perform these tasks more than their husbands. In fact, babies get used to it. The majority of infants and toddlers would rather call out for Mom's caring touch than Dad's. Your daughter is not only more interested in being comforted by Mom for the first few years; she likes to play more with a mom who is more attentive to all the nuances of her behavior.

Mothers are more interested in spending longer periods of time with their daughters. Utilizing her acute senses to stay attuned to her baby's needs, mothers are lighter sleepers when they have a baby in the house. Fathers are less likely to hear their daughter cry at night and are more likely to be annoyed if she awakens him.

Mommy Brain Story

From an early age, Susan had always enjoyed being the center of her peers' social scene. Ginny, her five-year-old daughter, was different. She was just as content being by herself as she was playing with other kids. One weekend, the preschool director's son was having his fifth birthday party and Ginny wasn't invited. It was Susan, not Ginny, who was devastated by the lack of an invitation. Susan made sure to have a very special play date set up for Ginny the afternoon of the party. Whether Ginny was aware the play date was scheduled during the same time as the party or not, Susan felt better making sure she wasn't alone the day of the party.

Mothers literally seem to have eyes in the back of their heads. At any given moment Mom is conscious of where her daughter is or what she needs. Unless specifically asked to keep an eye on his daughter, a father often assumes everything is fine.

Differences in Discipline

Mothers and fathers differ in the way they discipline their children. Some dads are quick to intervene, setting boundaries in a clear manner. Mom often interprets Dad's clarity as brusque and too harsh. Mothers often worry about how their child feels at the end of the discipline process. For mothers, getting the message across is often secondary to preserving her daughter's sense of self; fathers feel responsible for making sure the message is primary.

So What Are Two Loving Parents to Do?

- *Accept that you are different* and appreciate that these differences broaden your daughter's life experience. At times it is important to agree to disagree.
- *Give each other the opportunity to spend time alone with your daughter.* She needs both of you and both of you need time to practice being in charge. It's easy for fathers to turn over the parenting job to Mom if she happens to be around. If a mom isn't present, a dad really does know how to take care of his daughter.
- *Give yourself time alone without your daughter.* Your girl will be okay. It's important for a mom to learn how to take care of herself even when she becomes a mother!
- *Remember, before you were parents, you were a couple.* Fathers report feeling neglected by their wives, who put the kids

ahead of them. Take care of your relationship; it will sustain both of you over time.

- **Let dads roughhouse.** Dads know how to play physically with their children. Your girl will learn to appreciate the stimulation. Mothers often think Dad is over-stimulating their baby. Dad is in fact activating synapses and giving your girl an opportunity to explore other aspects of her world.

Where Else Can You Find Support?

You don't have to parent alone. Use your extended family, both biological and otherwise. Your parents, friends, and members of your support network all are there to support you. Ask questions; glean from the wisdom of their experience. You may not always agree with their advice, but an alternative perspective can be valuable.

The Expert Community

Experts can weigh in as well with parenting advice. The Gurian Institute is one of many organizations that you'll find invaluable in assisting you as a parent. On the Web site you will find recommendations for articles, additional Web sites, and books on brain research that will support you as you begin your parenting adventure. Find us at www.gurianinstitute.com. The Institute focuses on providing families with a crucial understanding of how boys and girls learn and grow differently.

Additionally, you'll find within your community any number of local and national organizations to help you with advice. There are literally millions of options. A quick check on the Internet resulted in 2,700,000 options when "parenting advice" was searched!

Whom do you listen to? Which option is a good fit for you and your family? After talking to your pediatrician and other supports, you and your spouse will in the end need to begin trusting yourselves.

A Special Note for Dads

Your daughter needs you. Even though the lion's share of early parenting tasks may fall to your wife, especially if she is breast-feeding, you play a significant role.

According to the American Academy of Pediatrics, "When fathers play a visible and nurturing role in their children's lives, the children have better emotional and social outcomes and are more likely to have stronger coping and adaptation skills, be better equipped to solve problems, stay in school longer, have longer-lasting relationships and have a higher work productivity."

A Special Note for Overworked, Exhausted Moms

Give up trying to be the super mom. There are no perfect moms. There are, however, "good enough" moms. Spend some time talking with other mothers and your husband about what you are willing to let go of. The house doesn't have to be perfect and you don't need to be back in your skinny jeans this month. Ask yourself what tasks you can share with your husband. And if he cleans the toilet bowl, are you willing to let him do it his way?

A Final Word

Nanette is a talented OB-GYN. She is married to a well-respected internist. The couple had Tanya, now five, while they were in their residency programs. Will, their second child, was born just last year.

One day, standing at the doctors' lab, Nanette confessed to her nurse that if she had done anything else seven days a week, twenty-four hours a day for five years, she would feel as if she had mastered the task. Parenting left her feeling chronically incompetent. Just when she felt like she understood what Tanya or Will needed and that she was on top of her mothering game, one or the other would reach a new developmental milestone, providing her with new challenges, requiring her to revisit her approach to parenting.

Nanette is not alone. There will be times when you will feel—just as she does—masterful and ready to give advice to other parents. Other times you will feel woefully inadequate. Just like your daughter, mothers and fathers go though phases. Give your daughter and yourself time. You are all under construction and we can assure you that with love, good humor, and mutual support, you'll all be able to deal with whatever happens next.

Sources

Introduction

Allen, J. S., & others. "Neuroscience for Kids: She Brains—He Brains." Society for Neuroscience. Retrieved from http://faculty.washington.edu/chudler/heshe.html.

Drubach, D. *The Brain Explained.* Upper Saddle River, N.J.: Prentice-Hall, 2000.

Eliot, L. *What's Going On in There? How the Brain and Mind Develop in the First Five Years of Life.* New York: Bantam Books, 1999.

Elium, J., & Elium, D. *Raising a Daughter.* Berkeley, Calif.: Celestial Arts, 2004.

"Gender and the Brain." *Brain Briefings.* Society for Neuroscience, 1998. Retrieved from www.sfn.org/briefings/gender.brain.html.

"Gender Differences." SlideShare. Retrieved from www.slideshare.net/readysetpresent/gender-differences-powerpoint.

Gurian, M. *The Wonder of Girls.* New York: Atria, 2002.

Laliberte, R. "The Difference Between Boys and Girls." *Parents,* Mar. 2006. Retrieved from www.parents.com/toddlers/development/behavioral/difference-between-boys-girls/.

LeVay, S. *The Sexual Brain.* Cambridge, Mass.: A Bradford Book, 1993.

Moir, A., & Jessel, D. *Brain Sex: The Real Difference Between Men and Women.* New York: Dell, 1989.

Sax, L. *Why Gender Matters.* New York: Doubleday, 2005.

Springer, S. P., & Deutsch, G. *Left Brain Right Brain* (4th ed.). New York: Freeman, 1993.

Chapter One

Achiron, R., Lipitz, S., & Achiron, A. "Sex-Related Differences in the Development of the Human Fetal Corpus Callosum." *Prenatal Diagnosis,* 2001, *21*(2), 116–120.

Allen, L. S., & Gorski, R. A. "Sexual Dimorphism of the Anterior Commissure and Massa Intermedia of the Human Brain. *Journal of Comparative Neurology,* 1991, *312,* 97–104.

Baron-Cohen, S. "Do Sex Differences in Empathy Account for Sex Differences in Language Acquisition?" *Coevolution of Language and Theory of Mind,* 2007. Retrieved Aug. 8, 2007, from http://www.interdisciplines.org/coevolution/papers/7/3.

Baron-Cohen, S., Luthmaya, S., & Knikmeyer, R. *Prenatal Testosterone in Mind: Amniotic Fluid Studies.* Cambridge, Mass.: MIT Press, 2004.

Becker, J. B., & others (eds.). *Sex Differences in the Brain: From Genes to Behavior.* New York: Oxford University Press, 2007.

Brizendine, L. *The Female Brain.* New York: Broadway Books, 2006.

Cahill, L. "His Brain, Her Brain." *Scientific American,* May 2005, pp. 40–47.

Chudler, E. "Neuroscience for Kids." 1996–2008. Retrieved July 23, 2007, from http://faculty.washington.edu/chudler/neurok.html.

de Lacoste, M., Holloway, R., & Woodward, D. "Sex Differences in the Fetal Human Corpus Callosum." *Human Neurobiology,* 1986, *5*(2), 93–96.

Goodwin, M. "Can I Choose My Baby's Sex?" *BabyCenter.* n.d. Retrieved from www.babycenter.com/404_can-i-choose-my -babys-sex_1933.bcA .

Graham, J. "Boosting Baby's Brain Before Birth." *Parents.com.* Sept. 2000. Retrieved Aug. 21, 2007, from www.parents.com/ parents/story.jsp?storyid=/Templatedata/parents/story/data/ 1001.xml.

Harvard School of Public Health. "Pregnant Women Carrying Boys Eat More Than Those Carrying Girls." Press Release. June 6, 2003. Retrieved Aug. 8, 2007, from www.hsph.harvard.edu /news/press-releases/archives/2003-releases/press06062003 .html.

Healy, J. M. *Your Child's Growing Mind.* New York: Broadway Books, 2004.

Hines, M. *Brain Gender.* New York: Oxford University Press, 2004.

Hopson, J. L. "Fetal Psychology." *Psychology Today,* Sept.-Oct. 1998, *31*(5), 44.

Human Genome Project. "20 Facts About the Human Genome." *Welcome Trust Sanger Institute,* Cambridge, England. Aug. 10, 2007. Retrieved from www.sanger.ac.uk/HGP/draft2000/ facts.shtml.

Ingemarsson, I. "Gender Aspects of Preterm Birth." *BJOG: An International Journal of Obstetrics and Gynecology,* 2003, 110.s20, 34–38.

Kimura, D. "Sex Differences in the Brain." SciAm.com. May 13, 2002. Retrieved Aug. 6, 2007, from www.sciam.com/article.cfm?id= 00018E9D-879D-1D06-8E49809EC588EEDF&page=1.

Marano, H. E. "The New Sex Scorecard." *Psychology Today,* July–Aug. 2003. Retrieved Aug. 2007, from http://psychologytoday .com/articles/PTO-20030624-000003.html.

Marsas, L. "He Thinks, She Thinks." *Discover.* July 5, 2007. Retrieved July 27, 2007, from http://discovermagazine.com/2007/brain/she-thinks.

Murkoff, H., Eisenberg, A., & Hathaway, S. *What to Expect the First Year.* New York: Workman, 2003.

"Pregnancy." *Medline Plus.* U.S. National Library of Medicine, National Institutes of Health. Jan. 2007. Retrieved Aug. 2007, from www.nlm.nih.gov/medlineplus/pregnancy.html.

"Prenatal Form and Function—The Making of an Earth Suit." The Endowment for Human Development, 2007. Retrieved Aug. 2007, from http://www.ehd.org/dev_article_intro.php.

Rosen, P. "Boy or Girl: Can You Choose?" *American Baby.* May 2005. Retrieved from www.parents.com/parents/story.jsp?page=2&storyid=/templatedata/ab/story/data/BoyOrGirl06152005.xml.

Villar, J., & others. "World Health Organization Randomized Trial of Calcium Supplementation Among Low Calcium Intake Pregnant Women." .*American Journal of Obstetrics and Gynecology,* 2006, *194*(3), 639–649.

Zeisel, S. "The Fetal Origins of Memory: The Role of Dietary Choline in Optimal Brain Development." *Journal of Pediatrics.* 2006, *149*(5), S131–S136.

Chapter Two

"Babies' Brain Development Immediately After Birth." *Medical News Today,* Dec. 29, 2003. Retrieved from www.medicalnewstoday.com/articles/5059.php.

BabyCenter Medical Advisory Board. "Help Your Child Understand Speech and Concepts." *BabyCenter,* n.d. Retrieved from www.babycenter.com/0_help-your-child-understand-speech-and-concepts_11734.bc.

Baron-Cohen, S. *The Essential Difference.* New York: Basic Books, 2003.

Baron-Cohen, S., Knickmeyer, R. C., & Belmonte, M. K. "Sex Differences in the Brain: Implications for Explaining Autism" *Science,* Nov. 4, 2005, *310*(5749), 819–823.

Brizendine, L. *The Female Brain.* New York: Broadway Books, 2006.

Caplan, F. *The First Twelve Months of Life.* New York: Bantam Books, 1984.

Cassidy, J., & Ditty, K. "Gender Differences Among Newborns on a Transient Otoacoustic Emissions Test for Hearing." *Journal of Music Therapy,* 2001, *37*, 28–35.

"Cognition Through the Lifespan." Retrieved from www.columbia .edu/itc/hs/nursing/n4225/2004_02/lect05Slides.pdf.

Cone-Wesson, B., & Ramirez, G. "Hearing Sensitivity in Newborns Estimated from ABRs to Bone-Conducted Sounds." *Journal of the American Academy of Audiology,* 1997, *8*, 299–307.

"Development of Cochlear Active Mechanisms in Humans Differs Between Gender." *Neuroscience.* Letters, 1996, *220*, 49–52.

Don, M., Ponton, C., Eggermont, J. J., & Masuda, A. "Gender Differences in Cochlear Response Time: An Explanation for Gender Amplitude Differences in the Unmasked Auditory Brainstem Response." *Journal of the Acoustical Society of America,* 1995, *94*, 2135–2146.

Eliot, L. *What's Going On in There? How the Brain and Mind Develop in the First Five Years of Life.* New York: Bantam Books,1999.

Frederikse, M., & others. "Sex Differences in the Inferior Parietal Lobe." *Cerebral Cortex,* 1999, *9*, 896–901.

"Gender and Pain." *Brain Briefings.* Society for Neuroscience, May 2007. Retrieved from www.sfn.org/index.cfm?pagename= brainBriefings_gender_ and_pain.

"Gender and the Brain." *Brain Briefings.* Society for Neuroscience, 1998. Retrieved from www.sfn.org/briefings/gender.brain .html.

"Gender Differences." SlideShare. Retrieved from www.slideshare .net/readysetpresent/gender-differences-powerpoint.

Green, A. "Masturbation in Young Children." Drgreene.com, 2007. Retrieved Sept. 14, 2007, from www.drgreene.com/21_606 .html.

Halpern, D. F. *Sex Differences in Cognitive Abilities.* Mahwah, N.J.: Erlbaum, 2000.

Healy, J. M. *Your Child's Growing Mind.* New York: Broadway Books, 2004.

Multnomah County Library. *Brain Development: Birth to Six.* n.d. Retrieved from www.multcolib.org/birthtosix/braindev .html.

NCHS United States Clinical Growth Chart. Retrieved from www.cdc .gov/nchs/about/major/nhanes/growthcharts/clinical_charts .htm.

"Newborn Brains Grow Vision and Movement Regions First." *Science Daily,* Feb. 13, 2007. Retrieved from www.science daily.com/releases/2007/02/070208131703.htm.

Robledo, S. J. "Developmental Milestone: Self-Care." *BabyCenter,* n.d. Retrieved from http://parentcenter.babycenter.com/ 0_developmental-milestone-self-care_63974.pc.

Sullivan, D. "Your 18-Month-Old's Social and Emotional Development: Making Friends." *BabyCenter,* n.d. Retrieved from www.babycenter.com/0_your-18-month-olds-social-and -emotional-development-making-f_1213792.bc.

Springer, S. P., & Deutsch, G. *Left Brain Right Brain* (4th ed.). New York: Freeman, 1993.

Chapter Three

ADDvance-ADD (ADHD) Checklist for Girls. Retrieved from www
.addvance.com/help/women/girl_checklist.html.

Ames, L. B., & Ilg, F. *Your Three-Year-Old: Friend or Enemy.* New
York: Dell, 1985.

BabyCenter Medical Advisory Board. "The ABCs of Toilet Training."
BabyCenter, Sept. 2006. Retrieved from www.babycenter.com/
0_the-abcs-of-toilet-training_4399.bc.

BabyCenter Medical Advisory Board. "Help Your Child Understand
Speech and Concepts." *BabyCenter,* n.d. Retrieved from www
.babycenter.com/0_help-your-child-understand-speech-and
-concepts_11734.bc.

BabyCenter Medical Advisory Board. "Toilet Training: What Works?"
Baby Center, n.d. Retrieved from www.babycenter.com/
0_toilet-training-what-works_4397.bc.

Baron-Cohen, S. *The Essential Difference.* New York: Basic Books, 2003.

Baron-Cohen, S., Knickmeyer, R. C., & Belmonte, M. K. "Sex
Differences in the Brain: Implications for Explaining Autism."
Science, Nov. 4, 2005, *310*(5749), 819–823.

Beighle, A., & others. "Children's Physical Activity During Recess
and Outside of School." *Journal of School Health,* Dec. 2006,
76(10), 516–520.

Bland, J. "About Gender: Sex Differences." Retrieved from www.
gender.org.uk/about/07neur/77_diffs.htm.

Blanton, R. E., & others. "Gender Differences in the Left Inferior
Frontal Gyrus in Normal Children." *NeuroImage,* 2004, *22,*
626–636.

Boyatzis, C., Chazan, E., & Ting, C. Z. "Preschool Children's
Decoding of Facial Emotions." *Journal of Genetic Psychology,*
1993, *154,* 375–382.

Boyd, H. "Gender Differences: First Grade." Education.com. www
.education.com/magazine/article/Gender_First_Grade/.

Bremner, J. D., & others. "Gender Differences in Cognitive and
Neural Correlates in Remembrance of Emotional Words."
Psychopharmacology Bulletin, 2001, *35*, 55–74.

Caplan, F. *The Second Twelve Months of Life*. New York: Bantam
Books, 1984.

De Bellis, M. D., & others. "Sex Differences in Brain Maturation
During Childhood and Adolescence." *Cerebral Cortex*, June
2001, *11*(6), 552–557.

de Courten-Myers, G. M. "The Human Cerebral Cortex: Gender
Differences in Structure and Function." *Journal of Neuropathology and Experimentalogy Neurology*, 1999, *58*(3), 217–226.

Duff, S. J., & Hampson, E. "A Sex Difference on a Novel Spatial
Working Memory Task in Humans." *Brain and Cognition*,
2001, *47*(3), 470–493.

Eals, M., & Silverman, I. "The Hunter-Gatherer Theory of Spatial
Sex Differences: Proximate Factors Mediating the Female
Advantage in Recall of Object Arrays." *Ethology and
Sociobiology*, 1994, *15*, 95–105.

Eliot, L. *What's Going On in There? How the Brain and Mind Develop
in the First Five Years of Life*. New York: Bantam Books, 1999.

Fales, E. "A Comparison of the Vigorousness of Play Activities of
Preschool Boys and Girls." *Child Development*, June, 1937,
8(2), 144–158.

"Frequently Asked Questions." n.d. Retrieved from www.totsand
toddlers.com/faq.

"Gender Differences in Language Appear Biological: Language
Processing More Abstract in Girls, More Sensory in Boys."

EurekAlert. Retrieved from www.eurekalert.org/pub_releases/ 2008-03/nu-gdi030308.php.

"Gender Differences in the Human Cerebral Cortex: More Neurons in Males; More Processes in Females." *Journal of Child Neurology,* 1999, *14*(2), 98–107.

Gibson, K. R. "Myelinisation and Behavioural Development: A Comparative Perspective on Questions of Neoteny, Altricity and Intelligence." In K. R. Gibson & A. C. Petersen (eds.), *Brain Maturation and Cognitive Development.* New York: Aldine De Gruyter, 1985.

"Girls' Learning Style. Girls Learning Differently." n.d. Retrieved from http:www.girlslearndifferently.com/learningstyles.html.

Gur, R. C., & others. "Sex Differences in Brain Gray and White Matter in Healthy Young Adults." *Journal of Neuroscience,* 1999, *19,* 4065–4972.

Gur, R. C., & others. "An fMRI Study of Sex Differences in Regional Activation to a Verbal and Spatial Task." *Brain and Language Journal,* 2000, *74,* 346–350.

Gryn, G., & others. "Brain Activation During Human Navigation: Gender-Different Neural Networks as Substrate of Performance." *Nature Neuroscience,* Apr. 2000, *3*(4), 404–408.

Gurian, M., & others. *Boys and Girls Learn Differently!* San Francisco: Jossey-Bass, 2001.

Haier, R. J., & others. "The Neuroanatomy of General Intelligence: Sex Matters." *Neuroimage,* 2005, *25,* 320–327.

Haines, C. "Sequencing, Co-Ordination and Rhythm Ability in Young Children." *Child Care, Health and Development,* Sept. 2003, *29*(5), 395–409.

Hall, J. A., & Matsumoto, D. "Gender Differences in Judgments of
   Multiple Emotions from Facial Expressions." *Emotion,* 2004,
   4, 201–206.

Halpern, D. F., & others. "The Science of Sex Differences in Science
   & Mathematics." *Psychological Science in the Public Interest,*
   Aug. 2001, *8*(1), 1–51.

Hanlon, H., Thatcher, R., & Cline, M. "Gender Differences in
   the Development of EEG Coherence in Normal Children."
   Developmental Neuropsychology, 1999, *16*(3), 479–506.

Harmel, K. "Language Delay and Gender." *American Baby,* Apr. 2004.
   Retrieved from www.parents.com/parents/story.jsp?storyid=/
   templatedata/ab/story/data/ABApr2004LanguageDelay_
   04212004.xml.

Healy, J. M. *Your Child's Growing Mind.* New York: Broadway Books,
   2004.

Hernandez, C. G., & others. *Primary Care Pediatrics.* Philadelphia:
   Lippincott Williams & Wilkins, 2007, p. 117.

Jarvis, P. "Rough and Tumble Play: Lessons in Life." *Evolutionary
   Psychology,* 2006, *4,* 330–346.

Johnson, L. A. "Behavior Drug Spending Up: More Kids Taking
   Pills for ADHD." *Associated Press,* May 17, 2004.

Kansaku, K., & Kitazawa, S. "Imaging Studies on Sex Differences
   in the Lateralization of Language." *Neuroscience Research,*
   2001, *41,* 333–337.

Karges-Bone, L. *More Than Pink and Blue: How Gender Can Shape
   Your Curriculum.* Carthage, Ill.: Teaching and Learning
   Company, 1998.

Karras, T. "Types of ADHD in Girls." *BabyCenter,* n.d. Retrieved
   from http://parentcenter.babycenter.com/0_types-of-adhd
   -in-girls_67350.pc

Kimura, D. "Sex Differences in the Brain." *Scientific American,* 1992, *10,* 118–125.

Kimura, D. *Sex and Cognition.* Cambridge, Mass.: MIT Press, 1999.

Kimura, D. "The Hidden Mind." *Cerebral Cortex,* June 2001, *11*(6), 552–557.

Klomsten, A. T., Skaalvik, E. M., & Espnes, G. A. "Physical Self Concept and Sports: Do Gender Differences Still Exist?" *Sex Roles: A Journal of Research.* Retrieved from http://goliath.ecnext.com/coms2/gi_0199-708695/Physical-self-concept-and-sports.html.

Labarthe, J. C. "Are Boys Better Than Girls at Building a Tower or a Bridge at 2 Years of Age?" *Archives of Diseases of Childhood,* 1997, *77,* 140–144.

Larson, J., & Gidley, C. "Effects of Gender and Age on Motor Exam in Typically Developing Children." *Developmental Neuropsychology,* 2007, *32*(1), 543–562.

Lawton, C. A., & Kallai, J. "Gender Differences in Wayfinding Strategies and Anxiety About Wayfinding: A Cross-Cultural Comparison." *Sex Roles: A Journal of Research,* Nov. 2002. Retrieved from http://findarticles.com/p/articles/mi_m2294/is_2002_Nov/ai_97728454.

Leahey, E. "Gender Differences in Mathematical Trajectories." *Social Forces,* 2001, *80,* 713–732.

Libby, M. N., & Aries, E. "Gender Differences in Preschool Children's Narrative Fantasy." *Psychology of Women Quarterly,* Sept. 1989, *13*(3), 203–306.

Luders, E., & others. "Gender differences in cortical complexity." *Nature Neuroscience,* 2000, *7,* 799–800.

McGinis, L., & others. "A Review of Gendered Consumption in Sport and Leisure." Retrieved from www.amsreview.org/articles/mcginnis05-2003.pdf.

McGivern, R. F., & others. "Gender Differences in Incidental Learning and Visual Recognition Memory: Support for a Sex Difference in Unconscious Environmental Awareness." *Personality and Individual Differences,* 1998, *25,* 223–232.

McKelvie, S. J., & others. "Gender Differences in Recognition Memory for Faces and Cars: Evidence for the Interest Hypothesis." *Bulletin of the Psychonomic Society,* 1993, *31,* 447–448.

Miller, K. "Gender Wars: Getting Boys and Girls to Play Together." *Parents.* Retrieved from www.parents.com/parents/story.jsp?storyid=/templatedata/parents/story/data/1150396041057.xml.

Multnomah County Library. *Brain Development: Birth to Six.* n.d. Retrieved from www.multcolib.org/birthtosix/braindev.html.

Ostrov, J. M., & Keating, C. F. "Gender Differences in Preschool Aggression During Free Play and Structured Interactions: An Observational Study." *Social Development,* 2004, *13*(2), 255–277.

Rabinowicz, T., & others. "Structure of the Cerebral Cortex in Men and Women." *Journal of Neuropathology and Experimental Neurology,* Jan. 2002, *61*(1), 46–57.

"Research Summary—Gender in Education. Differences Between Boys and Girls." Learning About Learning. Retrieved from www.ltscotland.org.uk/learningaboutlearning/differences/research/rsgenderineducation.asp .

Rhoads, S. E. *Taking Sex Differences Seriously.* San Francisco: Encounter Books, 2004.

Ripley, A. "Who Says a Woman Can't Be Einstein?" *Time,* Mar. 7, 2005, *165*(10), 55.

Robledo, S. J. "Developmental Milestone: Self-Care." *BabyCenter,* n.d. Retrieved from http://parentcenter.babycenter.com/0_developmental-milestone-self-care_63974.pc.

Sandstrom, N., Kaufman, J., & Huettel, S. A. "Males and Females Use Different Distal Cues in a Virtual Environment Navigation Task." *Cognitive Brain Research,* 1998, *6,* 351–360.

Saucier, D., & others. "Are Sex Differences in Navigation Caused by Sexually Dimorphic Strategies or by Differences in the Ability to Use the Strategies?" *Behavioral Neuroscience,* 2002, *116,* 403–410.

Schum, T., & others. "Sequential Acquisition of Toilet-Training Skills: A Descriptive Study of Gender and Age Differences in Normal Children." *Pediatrics,* Mar. 3, 2002, *109*(3), e48.

"Sex, Sexual Orientation and Sex Hormones Influence Human Cognitive Function." *Current Opinion in Neurobiology,* 1996, *6,* 259–263.

Shaywitz, B. A., & others. "Sex Differences in the Functional Organization of the Brain for Language." *Nature,* Feb. 16, 1995, *373,* 607–609.

Shechter, S., & others. "Gender Differences in Apparent Motion Perception." *Perception,* 1991, *20*(3), 307–314.

Sherar, L. B. "Age and Gender Differences in Youth Physical Activity: Does Physical Maturity Matter?" *Medicine and Science in Sports and Exercise,* 2007, *39*(5), 830–835.

"Structural Brain Variation and General Intelligence." *NeuroImage,* 2004, *23,* 425–433.

Sullivan, D. "Your 18-Month-Old's Social and Emotional Development: Making Friends." *BabyCenter.* n.d. Retrieved from www.babycenter.com/0_your-18-month-olds-social -and-emotional-development-making-f_1213792.bc.

Tannick, M. "Young Children's Rough and Tumble Play: Observations of Five Year Old Play." Retrieved from www.csuchico .edu/kine/tasp/06prespapers/tannockroughtumbleplay paper.ppt.

Thayer, J. F., & Johnsen, B. H. "Sex Differences in Judgment of Facial Affect: A Multivariate Analysis of Recognition Errors." *Scandinavian Journal of Psychology,* Sept. 2000, *41*(3), 243–246.

"Toddler's First Steps: A 'Best Chance' Guide to Parenting Your Six-Month- to Three-Year-Old." Retrieved from www.health.gov .bc.ca/cpa/publications/firststeps.pdf.

Vaughn, B. E., & others. "Negative Interactions and Social Competence for Preschool Children in Two Samples: Reconsidering the Interpretation of Aggressive Behavior for Young Children." *Merrill-Palmer Quarterly,* 2003, *49,* 518–521.

Weiman, H. "Gender Differences in Cognitive Functioning." Retrieved from http://homepages.luc.edu/~hweiman/GenderDiffs.html.

Willmer, J., & Nakayama, K. "A Large Gender Difference in Smooth Motion Pursuit." *Journal of Vision, 6*(6), Abstract 94, 94a.

Wilson, K. "Development of Conflicts and Conflict Resolution Among Preschool Children." *Canadian Journal of Education,* Winter 1997, *22*(1), 33–45.

"With Boys and Girls in Mind." *Educational Leadership.* Nov. 2004, *62*(3), 21–28.

Wood, G., & Shors, T. J. "Stress Facilitates Classical Conditioning in Males, But Impairs Classical Conditioning in Females Through Activational Effects of Ovarian Hormones." *Proceedings of the National Academy of Sciences,* 1998, *95,* 4066–4071.

Yark, F. "Gender Differences Are Real." *Narth.* Feb. 2008. Retrieved from www.narth.com/docs/york.html.

Chapter Four

Abrams, D. C. "The Making of a Modern Dad." *Psychology Today,* Mar. 2002, pp. 38–47.

Berg, S. J., & Wynne-Edwards, K. E. "Changes in Testosterone, Cortisol, and Estradiol Levels in Men Becoming Fathers." *Mayo Clinic Proceedings,* 2001, *76,* 582–592.

Blum, D. *Sex on the Brain: The Biological Differences Between Men and Women.* New York: Penguin Books, 1998.

Cahill, L. "Why Sex Matters for Neuroscience?" *Nature Reviews Neuroscience,* 2006, *7,* 477–484.

Carey, B. "Men and Women Really Do Think Differently." *Live Science,* Jan. 20, 2005. Retrieved from www.livescience.com/health/050120_brain_sex.html.

Couzin, J. "A 'His' or 'Hers' Brain Structure." *Science Now Daily News,* Apr. 7, 2006.

Diamond, M. "Male and Female Brains: Lecture for Women's Forum." *West Annual Meeting,* San Francisco, Calif., 2003.

Eisler, R., & Levine, D. S. "Nurture, Nature and Caring: We Are Not Prisoners of Our Genes." *Brain and Mind,* 2002, *3,* 9–52.

Ellison, K. *The Mommy Brain: How Motherhood Makes Us Smarter.* New York: Basic Books, 2005.

Gray, P. B., & others. "Marriage and Fatherhood Associated with Lower Levels of Testosterone." *Evolution and Human Behavior,* 2002, *23,* 193–201.

Gurian, M. *Nurture the Nature: Understanding and Supporting Your Child's Unique Core Personality.* San Francisco: Jossey-Bass, 2007.

Jovanovic, H. "PET Evaluation of Central Serotonergic Neuro-Transmission in Women." Doctoral thesis. Feb. 29, 2008. Retrieved from http://diss.kib.ki.se/2008/978-91-7357-510-2/thesis.pdf.

LeVay, S. *The Sexual Brain.* Cambridge, Mass.: A Bradford Book, 1993.

Lemoick, M. "The Chemistry of Desire." *Time,* Jan. 12, 2004, *163*(3), 68–72.

Marsa, L. "He Thinks, She Thinks." *Discover,* July 5, 2007. Retrieved from http://discovermagazine.com/2007/brain/she-thinks.

Moir, A., & Jessel, D. *Brain Sex: The Real Difference Between Men & Women.* New York: Dell, 1989.

Moir, A., & Moir, B. *Why Men Don't Iron.* New York: Citadel, 1999.

Mlyniec, V. "What a Son and a Daughter Need from a Mom." *Parents.com.* Retrieved from www.parents.com/parents/story.jsp?page=2&storyid=/templatedata/fc/story/data/1128972070434.xml.

Onion, A. "Sex in the Brain: Research Showing Men and Women Differ in More Than One Area." *ABC News,* Sept. 21, 2004.

Palmer, L. "Bonding Matters: The Chemistry of Attachment." *Attachment Parenting International News,* 2002, 5(2).

Pease, B., & Pease, A. *Why Men Don't Listen and Women Can't Read Maps.* New York: Broadway Books, 2000.

"Research in Gender and Brain Suggests Differences at Cell Level." *Society for Neuroscience,* Oct. 17, 2006. Retrieved from www.sfn.org/index.cfm?pagename=news_101706b

Sabbatini, R. "Are There Differences Between the Brains of Males and Females?" *Brain and Mind,* n.d. Retrieved from www.cerebromente.org.br/n11/mente/eisntein/cerebro-homens.html.

Schulz, M. L. *The New Feminine Brain.* New York: Free Press, 2005.

Sousa, D. A. *How the Brain Learns* (2nd ed.). Thousand Oaks, Calif.: Corwin Press, 2001.

Stossel, J. "Boys and Girls Are Different: Men, Women, and the Sex Difference." ABC News Special, Jan. 17, 1998, transcript from the Internet, The Electric Library.

Resources for Parents of Girls

In a world filled with constant input from the Internet and media, how does a parent choose what to read, view, or listen to?

We've done some preliminary filtering for you. Start here. You'll find further suggestions at these sites, or from your pediatrician, your friends, and family.

Book Ideas for Moms and Dads

The Wonder of Girls, by Michael Gurian.

The Daring Book for Girls, by Miriam Peskowitz.

Raising a Daughter: Parents and the Awakening of a Healthy Woman, by Jeanne and Don Elium.

What to Expect the First Year (2nd ed.), by Arlene Eisenberg.

The Girls Book: How to Be the Best at Everything, by Juliana Foster.

T. Berry Brazelton, a noted pediatrician, has a number of books about infants, toddlers, sleep, and building a family. Two of his more recent publications include: *Touchpoints Birth to Three: Your Child's Emotional and Behavioral Development* and *The Irreducible Needs of Children: What Every Child Must Have to Grow.*

William Dougherty, family therapist, has written *The Intentional Family: Simple Rituals to Strengthen Family Ties,* a book that offers simple suggestions to build a family.

Great Books for Girls: More Than 600 Books to Inspire Today's Girls and Tomorrow's Women, edited by Kathleen Odean.

Help with Mothering

Mother-Daughter Project: How Mothers and Daughters Can Band Together, Beat the Odds, and Thrive Through Adolescence, by SuEllen Hamkins, MD, and Ren~EAe Schultz, MA. This book and its companion Web site helps mothers develop mother-daughter groups.

Dad Support

Strong Fathers, Strong Daughters: 10 Secrets Every Father Should Know, by Meg Meeker.

Fathers and Daughters home page for father-daughter relationships at www.fathermag.com.

Check out the October 2002 issue of *Parents Magazine* for an introduction to Fatherhood 101 in an article by David Sparrows, "Bonding with Baby."

Help for Your Relationship

John Gottman has written several books applying biological research to relationships, including *Seven Principles for Making Marriages Work,* Three Rivers/Random House, 1999.

Also check out Michael Gurian's *What Could He Be Thinking?* St. Martins, 2004.

Why Talking Is Not Enough: Eight Loving Actions That Will Transform Your Marriage, by Susan Page. Jossey-Bass, 2007.

The Secrets of Happily Married Women: How to Get More Out of Your Relationship by Doing Less, by Scott Haltzman, MD, Theresa Foy DiGeronimo. Jossey-Bass, 2008.

The Secrets of Happily Married Men: Eight Ways to Win Your Wife's Heart Forever, by Scott Haltzman, MD, with Theresa Foy DiGeronimo. Jossey-Bass, 2007.

Books for Your Girl

Every year wonderful new books are published for toddlers and pre-schoolers. Here are a few new ones and some well-loved classics.

The Secret Science Project That Almost Ate the School, by Judy Sierra, Simon & Schuster, 2006, is a favorite for both boys and girls.

George and Martha, written and illustrated by James Marshall, Houghton Mifflin, 2008, features two plump hippos and the delicacy with which they respect each other's feelings.

Chester's Way, by Kevin Henkes, HarperTrophy, 1997, features Lilly the mouse as one of the bravest, most flamboyant young females around. She rescues her friends from bullies, teaches them how to do wheelies, and always carries a loaded squirt gun.

Jojo's Flying Side Kick, by Brian Pinckney, Aladdin, 1998. In order to earn her yellow belt in Tae Kwon Do, young JoJo must break a board with a flying side kick. With the help of her family, she masters her fears and succeeds.

The Adventures of Isabel, by Ogden Nash, Trumpet Club, 1992. In this funny poem, Isabel conquers a bear, a witch, a giant, a doctor, and a nightmare. The pictures will make your girl laugh while Nash's poetry will help her learn to banish her own nightmares.

Lon Po Po: A Red-Riding Hood Story from China, Putnam Juvenile, 1996. Exquisite illustrations accompany this Chinese folktale about a young girl who outwits a nasty wolf and saves her sisters.

Eloise Kay Thompson's *Eloise,* Simon & Schuster, 1969, tears around the Plaza Hotel in New York, driving adults crazy and having a terrific time.

Robert Munsch's *The Paper Bag Princess,* Annick Press, 1992. This princess outsmarts a dragon who has destroyed her kingdom, burned all her clothes, and carried off her prince. And when the dragon is vanquished, she tells him what for and then dances off into the sunset.

Movies, TV, and Your Girl

Under age two, talking, singing, reading, listening to music, or playing are far more important to your daughter's development than any TV or movie. Brain research supports the American Academy of Pediatrics position that parents need to limit TV and movie viewing for toddlers and preschoolers. Be selective in choosing your daughter's first movies.

Before watching a movie with your preschooler check out the following site for advice on movies and your preschooler:

www.pbs.org/parents/childrenandmedia/tvmovies-preschool.html

And then enjoy a few of our favorites:

The Incredibles tells the story of some over-the-hill superheroes whose kids get to be superheroes in their own story. This is a favorite for both parent and child.

Mulan. When her father cannot serve in the military, a young girl disguises herself as a man to save the day.

Pocahontas. The story of a capable woman who can talk to birds, save her tribe, and fall in love.

Charlotte's Web. A classic, with a girl protagonist who's not afraid of bugs or pigs.

Mary Poppins. A strong woman whips a stuffy family into shape through laughter and play

And once you tuck your girl in, grab a cup of tea and watch our favorite movie for moms and dads, *Parenthood* starring Steve Martin.

Support and Information on the Web

With hundreds of thousands of Internet sites devoted to parenting concerns, there's an overabundance of information available to you. Following are a few suggestions to get you started:

The Gurian Institute assists parents in finding practical solutions to real-life parenting dilemmas using the most recent scientific research. You can access the Institute at www.gurianinstitute.com. The Institute provides resources and services through four divisions: Families, Education, Corporate, and Human Services. Parents may subscribe to the Institute's preschool newsletter for parents by clicking on the family link.

www.brainconnection.com provides cutting-edge information on brain development throughout the lifespan, with particular attention devoted to education and problem solving.

www.drgreene.com is a general pediatrics site with good common-sense advice.

A parent cooperative preschool is organized by a group of families with similar philosophies who hire a trained consultant-teacher.

Parents gain insight into child behavior by observing other children. Children participate in a supervised play and learning experience with children of their own age, while parents and children develop an extended family with friendships they carry throughout their lives. Find out more about this built-in community at www .preschools.coop/home.htm.

www.kidsindanger.com keeps parents current on product safety concerns.

www.kidshealth.org is an all-encompassing site that appeals to parents, kids, and teens, providing practical parenting information, homework help, teen advice, straight talk from professionals throughout the world, as well as doctor-approved health information about kids from birth through adolescence.

Information from the American Academy of Pediatrics can be found at www.aap.org.

http://userpages.umbc.edu/~korenman/wmst/links_girls.html. This Web site lists Web sites focusing on girls' or young women's interests and resources. A red asterisk indicates a site designed *for* girls or young women, rather than a site for adults *about* girls or young women.

If you have specific mental health concerns about your daughter, consult:

www.ncld.org, a site which provides parents with information about learning disabilities, their warning signs, and resources to contact.

The Web site for the National Institute of Mental Health found at www.nimh.nih.gov/health also has information on both autism and hyperactivity.

The Gurian Institute

If you would like to help your community better meet the developmental needs of both boys and girls, please contact the Gurian Institute. The Institute works with parents, schools, business corporations, the juvenile and adult corrections systems, medical and mental health professionals, and others who serve children and adults.

Gurian Institute staff and trainers provide training and regional conferences, working throughout the United States, as well as in Canada and abroad. The Institute provides resources and services through four divisions: Families, Education, Corporate, and Human Services. Each can be accessed through www.gurianinstitute.com.

The Institute is committed to providing both science-based information and practical and relevant applications for everyday life. We help build self-sufficiency in communities. We believe that alone, each parent and each professional is a visionary; at the same time, by working together, we become the protective and successful social force our children and families most need.

To learn more, please visit www.gurianinstitute.com.

About the Authors

Stacie Bering, MD, is a board-certified obstetrician-gynecologist who practiced and taught obstetrics and gynecology for twenty-five years in Spokane, Washington. Health issues led to her second board certification in hospice and palliative medicine. She is now the medical director of an inpatient palliative medicine service for Empire Health Services in Spokane. She shares her precious free time skiing and traveling with her husband, Jeffry, and grown children Cassie and Zack in Spokane.

Adie Goldberg, ACSW, MEd, is a board-certified social worker who has worked in many clinical and university settings. She has been a psychiatric social worker at WomanHealth, an OB-GYN practice, for twenty years. This collaborative medical–social work practice model has received national attention. Eight years ago she began working as a Jewish education director at Temple Beth Shalom, and as part of this work, became a certified Gurian Institute Trainer. She utilizes gender brain concepts in both educational and clinical settings. Adie presents at local and national conventions on a broad range of topics and writes for both social work and Jewish journals on family, education, and spirituality issues. She is almost an empty nester with two adult daughters, Emily and Maggie, and a third daughter, Chloe, who is in high school. Adie can be reached at www.gurianinstitute.com.

Index

and overworked, exhausted
moms, 110
Synapses, 28, 101, 104, 109;
auditory, 41; creating, 63–64

T

Talking, 82
Tantrums and frustration, 88–89
Taste: breast feeding and,
41–42; buds, 42, 43; development of, 44; how baby girl
experiences, 41–42; variety
and, 43; workings of, 43
Television, 41, 50, 72, 78,
132–133
Temporal lobe, 39
Testosterone, 6, 9, 16–19, 99,
102–104; and autism, 83;
cigarettes and, 27; hits, 32;
and language, 81
Texture, detecting, 37
Thyroid, 26
Toddler and preschool years.
See Girls, toddler and preschool years
Toilet training, 89–90
Touch, 35, 94; baby girl experience of, 45–46; in cogni-
tive development, 80; and
comfort, 46; developing,
44; girl's sense of, 45; and

vasopressin, 103; working
of, 51–52
Toxemia, 25
Triple screen blood test, 13

U

Ultrasound test, 2, 12, 13
Uterus, 17, 26

V

Vagina, 17, 18, 57, 58, 90, 91
Vasopressin, 103
Verbal skills, 47
Videos, 41, 50
Vision, 74, 78, 79
Visual Discrimination, 79
Visual-spatial relation skills, 52
Vocabulary, 81, 82
Vulva, 57, 58

W

Wernicke's area, 49, 81
Whitaker, C., 98
Wolffian ducts, 17

X

X chromosomes, 5, 15–16
XX chromosomes, 15–16, 32

Y

Y chromosomes, 15, 16, 18, 20